SUSTAINABLE LIVING

Practical Eco-Friendly Tips for Green Living and Self-Sufficiency in the 21st Century
[Special Edition Collection]

By
Sustainable Stevie

Disclaimer
All information in this book has been carefully researched and
checked for factual accuracy. However, the author and publisher
make no warranty, express or implied, that the information
contained herein is appropriate for every individual, situation, or
purpose, and assumes no responsibility for errors or omissions.
The reader assumes the risk and full responsibility for all actions,
and the author and publisher will not be held responsible for any
loss or damage, whether consequential, incidental, special, or
otherwise that may result from the information presented in this
publication.

I have relied on my own experience as well as many different
sources for this book and have done my best to check facts and to
give credit where it is due; including helpful website addresses for
the reader's further research into a subject matter on his/her own. I
do not endorse nor assume any responsibility for the content on
remote websites as they frequently move or disappear.
Livesmartinfo.com is sometimes referenced within most chapters
to show what is currently available on Amazon for the related
subject matter. While all references to remote sites are checked
on a regular basis to confirm their continued existence, the author
and publisher have no control over, and cannot be responsible for,
the availability or content of remote websites.

First Printing, 2012

ISBN-13: 978-1475129571

ISBN-10: 1475129572

Printed in the United States of America

Table of Contents

INTRODUCTION

Particularly in the western world, the trend is that our lives are going in the direction of a more "green", organic, and eco-friendly way of living. Sustainability is now taken into consideration when making decisions for our families.

During the 20th century, there were many different inventions too numerous to mention here. Advancement has been made in phenomenal ways to make our lives more convenient and efficient. However, along with those advancements have come overuse, misuse, abuse, greed, etc. Basically, it's catching up with us if it hasn't already caught up with us.

The information in this book is aimed at bringing awareness to as many people as possible about how they can play their role individually toward a cleaner, eco-friendly environment which in turn benefits other species that share our planet. It must start with us.

If you take a look at each chapter's title, it is extremely broad by design. So despite your age group, there's something everyone can do. In other words, in one way or another we can each take personal action to a sustainable way of living.

Some of the topics might be something that you haven't given much thought to or might not even know about. So this is a good way to be informed and broaden your knowledge about green alternatives and other aspects of sustainability.

You've probably noticed other books that mention saving money or getting rich as a byproduct of going green or living sustainably. That basically comes down to recycling bad-for-the-environment electronic devices that some companies will actually pay you for, or choosing to buy used instead of new, or the use of natural products (for cleaning or gardening) that's abundantly available and more cost effective than a commercial brand of something, or reducing utility expenses through the use of solar energy, etc. These things and so much more are covered in this book including magnetic electricity and hybrid electric vehicles. There's even a chapter for natural baby products and as well as sustainable feminine hygiene alternatives.

This is one of those books that you save and refer back to like a reference guide. For those that have a particular interest in a specific topic, websites and sources that provide further details are cited. After reading through it, not only will you have a keen awareness about what is involved with going green, but you might also find yourself changing the way you do things for a more sustainable way of life!

CHAPTER ~1~

eCYCLING -
YOUR CONTRIBUTION TO A
GREEN ENVIRONMENT

With all the never ending electronic gadgetry that many of us own, especially in the western world as I like to call it, you can only imagine what it must be doing to the landfills and of course our environment. This book would not be complete without a chapter on how to do our part when it comes to eCycling and being a responsible user of electronics.

"With newer, more hi-tech electronics continuously becoming available to fit our lifestyles, we are replacing older models at rapid rates with no signs of slowing down. As a result, electronics are becoming one the fastest growing

portions of America's trash." - *Environmental Protection Agency*

There will be numerous references to useful programs, organizations and related products that will help you to play your role in such an important responsibility. Many practical tips will be shared that makes it easy to go green with your electronic devices and keep money in your pocket.

What is eCycling?

The term "eCycling" is very appropriate for the 21st century lifestyle (and the latter 20th century too). "E" stands for electronics and when you think of "cycling" what comes to mind is a circle, recycling, reusable; not leaving the loop. So eCycling means to recycle your old or unused electronic waste instead of throwing it away, thus contributing toxic waste in landfills.

You may be tempted to throw that old video game system, broken computer, and printer cartridges into the garbage can. But before you conveniently do that, consider this: The world generates 20 – 50 tons of e-waste every year and only 11.4% of that is recovered for recycling. That's astounding!

Sources that PAY YOU for recycling used electronics

There are people and companies out there that will pay you for recycling used electronics such as phones, computers, cameras, calculators, mp3 players, printers, video game systems, TVs, and more. You can get cash (or store credit) for it all. It should be noted that how much cash you get will depend on how new the item is and the condition it's in. Sites worth checking out include: BuyMyTronics.com, FlipSwap.com, Gazelle.com, and NextWorth.com. There's also EcoATM.com/ which specifically accepts used cell phones, iPods and MP3 players. They will ascertain the value and give you a gift card or in-store trade up. You can trade items for free at Freecycle.org.

Other recycling options

Don't forget about your cell phone service provider or your television manufacturer because they all have some kind of recycling program that uses old parts, batteries, and sometimes they have a charitable organization that they donate to. Visit your manufacturer's website to see what types of programs they offer.

If you don't prefer that route, simply call or stop by the store that you bought your electronic device from and see if they have a recycling program or can recommend one to you.

Donation of electronic devices

Although you might not get cash for that VCR from the 80s, or the computer monitor with a cracked screen, you can still recycle old and broken items. Contact your city or county recycling coordinator or go to Earth911.com, eiae.org (The Electronic Industries Alliance) and TechSoup.org. Use their search engine to find out where you can recycle electronics near you.

Something that happens in my area

Every quarter or so in my area, there's a sign posted somewhere in the parking lot of a close-by shopping center that advertises specific dates when you can drop off any kind of electronic device that you want to get rid of. They will be responsible for recycling it (or whatever they do with it). The point is that it's off your hands and your conscience.

An important tip specifically for cell phones

Be sure to remove your SIM card before doing any eCycling (donating, selling, trading, recycling etc.) because you don't want anyone accessing your cell phone's private information. If you're not sure how to remove it, contact your cell phone manufacturer's user manual. You might also try using third-party software that will completely and safely erase your phone records. Or try searching the Internet for how to remove SIM cards from that particular model phone.

A similar tip specifically for computers

Erase your computer's hard drive. This makes it empty again without any programs, software, or information that you had on it. Of course make sure you've already copied or saved that information onto an external hard drive or a different computer. If you're not sure how to do this, follow the same suggestions mentioned above. You might even ask a friend. Worst case scenario, take it to a computer service center and ask them to do it for you.

Alarming Statistics

- Electronics thrown in the trash (and not e-cycled) make up 70% of all hazardous waste!
- It takes 529 pounds of fossil fuels, 49 pounds of chemicals, and 1.5 tons of water to make one new, 53-pound, desktop computer system (including monitor)!
- Americans tossed 3 million tons of electronics into the trash, in 2006.

- E-waste (electronic waste) rises approximately 8% per year.

11 Common Items That Can Be eCycled

- Cell Phones
- Pagers
- Computer Hard Drives
- Keyboards
- Monitors
- Printers
- Scanners
- Televisions
- VCRs
- DVD Players
- Digital Equipment

eCycling Cell Phones

From the list above (not in any particular order), which electronic device do you think is prevalently found in landfills?

Yes, the first one - cell phones! Taking that into consideration and knowing that most of us have a cell phone these days, I'm going to really focus on the reality of cell phones.

There are more than 700 million cell phones used in the US today and at least 140 million of those cell phone users will ditch their current phone for a new phone every 14-18 months. I'm not one of those people who just "must" have the latest iPhone or e-gadget. Actually, I use my cell phone until the battery no longer holds a decent charge. At that point, it's time. So I figure I'll just get a replacement battery - not! I'm told that battery is no longer made and the phone is no longer manufactured because there's newer technology and better features in the latest phones. That's a typical justification. The phone wasn't even that old; what - maybe a little over one year? I'm just one example. Can you imagine how many countless other people have that same scenario? No wonder cell phones take the lead when it comes to "e-waste", another appropriate term.

The good news is that with all the features of touch-phones today, it eliminates the need for other electronics in your life. A lot of phones have alarm clocks, mp3 players, GPS systems, video and camera capabilities, calculators, calendars, notepads, and even the options to do banking and shopping. That eliminates 6 electronic gadgets, saves some paper, and saves you gas money. How awesome is that? Consider how wise you are by using your current phone and saving money because of doing that.

Just another little tidbit

Similar to all electronics, cell phones are made from highly engineered materials and most of it can be reused or repurposed. However, the battery contains toxic substances really bad for landfills.

Here's an *awesome* tip that stands alone for preserving your cell phone if you've ever dropped it

Have you ever had the misfortune of dropping your phone in water, or leaving it out in the rain? It probably won't work (or even turn on) and you may think you need to rush out and buy a new phone. There is actually a really cool fix for this problem. Remove the back of the phone and take out the battery. Put the phone and the battery in a sealed container of uncooked rice. Make sure there is enough rice in the container to fully cover the phone and the battery. Let it sit overnight (or 8-12 hours). By the next day, your phone should be dry and working with no problems!

What's the deal with cell phone chargers?

When plugged in, only 5% of the power consumed by a cell phone charger is used to actually charge the phone. The other 95% of power is consumed when the charger is plugged into the wall and not charging anything (phantom power). Always remember to unplug your cell phone charger when you're not using it!

7 Simple Things You Can Start Doing Right Now to Prolong the Life of Your Cell Phone

1. **When not in use, turn off your phone.** This includes when you're at the movie theater, or in an airplane. Cell phone use is restricted in both places anyway, so why waste the power and energy?
2. **Ditch the animated wallpaper/screen saver.** As cool as it looks, it still uses a lot of energy and considering the phone probably spends more time in your pocket or purse, why waste power on a screen saver you won't even be watching most of the time?
3. **Minimize the amount of time the phone's backlight remains on and reduce the brightness of it, if possible.**
4. **Use one of the simple ringtones that comes with your phone.** Vibrate and musical ringtones tend to use a lot more power and let's be honest, when is the last time you heard a cell phone ring that actually sounded like a phone, instead of a Katy Perry song or movie soundtrack?
5. **If you like to wear a headset, use a corded one instead of the wireless Bluetooth option.** Corded headsets consume less energy, and you

won't look like some crazy person talking to yourself.

6. Keep your phone clean. Every so often, turn off your phone and wipe down the screen, keys, and remove the back and clean the inside and battery. Dust and debris can sometimes shorten battery life, so ensuring your phone is clean will help keep it in top condition.

7. Only charge your phone when necessary. It may be a habit to plug in your phone every night before you go to bed, but that's a very wasteful habit. A lot of phones these days can keep their battery charged for a couple days at least. As long as you don't overuse phone features that drain battery power (like video, internet, and photos), you should only charge your phone every few days, when the battery is actually going dead.

eCycling Computers

3 statistics you should be aware of:

1. There are at least 300 million obsolete computers in the US today.

2. 81% of a desktop computer's total lifetime energy consumption goes towards just making the product.

3. At least 50% of a computer can be recycled today. The rest, however, ends up in landfills.

Did you know that most of the money you spend on your computer is going right down the drain? Of all the money you spend on powering your computer, only 15% of that goes towards when the computer is being used; the other 85% is wasted when your computer is idling (turned on, but not being used). Another scary thing about computers is the manufacturing of computer parts uses more water, fossil fuels, energy, toxic chemicals, and elemental gases than any other industry. That doesn't make them sound too eco-friendly now, does it?

6 Simple Things You Can Start Doing Right Now to Reduce Your Computer's Energy Consumption and Make it More Eco-Friendly

1. Turn off the screen saver. Like cell phones, screen savers can consume a lot of unnecessary energy.

2. If you're not going to be using the computer for a few hours or more, shut it down. This also includes connected devices, like speakers and printers. You should also plug everything into a power strip and flip the switch off to cut any phantom power that would be consumed otherwise.

3. If you do need to leave the computer on for a while, set it to hibernate, sleep, or standby. Be sure to check out other power-saving options that might come with your computer, as they can be programmed to automatically shut down your computer or set it to hibernate after a specific length of time. These settings allow you to keep your computer on and programs open, but will consume a lot less energy while you're away.

4. While you are using the computer, make the screen only as bright as you need it to be.

5. If you need to get a new computer, buy a laptop instead of a desktop. They consume less than 50% of the electricity that a desktop computer does. You should also look into computers made from recycled parts, or even used computers.

6. If you've had your computer for a while, you may notice that it runs slower than when you first bought it. Run the virus checker, disk cleanup, system error checking, and disk defragmenter programs to help speed things up a

bit. You should also clear your browser's history and cache, empty your recycle bin, and delete/remove any programs or files that you may not use very often. If you have a desktop computer, it is also a good idea to open it up once in a while (either via a side or back panel on the tower) and clean out the dust that has most likely accumulated in there.

eCycling Electronic Devices in General

1. What is Phantom Power?

Phantom Power is the power your electronic devices use when they are plugged in, but not turned on. This includes your TV, computer, and even your cell phone charger which all consumes energy, even when you're not using them. In fact, 40% of the energy used for your home electronics is when they are turned off. That's a lot of energy and money you are wasting on devices that aren't even in use!

The solution:

Well, you could unplug every single electronic device in your home when not in use (not counting appliances, like the fridge or oven). However, that can be very tedious and difficult for some, especially if there is a large piece of furniture blocking the wall outlet. Anything that has a bulky, AC-like adapter plug is especially prone to draining energy.

A much simpler solution:

Power strips. Buy some power strips and plug your devices into that, instead of the wall. When you're done using the computer, watching TV, or charging your phone, just flip the switch on the power strip. This allows you to keep things plugged in, but cuts any phantom power they'd normally consume. If you are the forgetful type, try using "smart" power strips. Even if you forget to flip the switch, they will automatically detect when plugged in items are not in use, and will cut off the phantom power for you. Pretty cool, huh?

2. Electronic Device Chargers (Solar, Wind and Hand Crank)

Many electronic products come with chargers, either for batteries or the product itself. In fact, right now, there are at least 1.5 billion chargers (or power adapters) in use in the US. Their total combined electricity makes up 11% of the national electric bill. It's these very chargers that are highly responsible for energy wasted on phantom power (mentioned in this chapter).

Eco-friendly options available today!

You don't need to use one of those big, bulky adapter plugs anymore. You can actually charge many devices with renewable energy (solar and wind), or even manual power. The awesome thing about these new chargers is they allow you to charge items on the go! They have skins for iPhones that double as solar chargers.

Check out wind chargers at www.livesmartinfo.com/windturbinechargers to see what they look like on Amazon. You can attach it to your bike, and they're even developing a dance charger. If you love to dance, that charger will be perfect for you. The battery is charged by your dancing and then that battery can be used to power your electronic devices. Pretty neat, huh?

Has this ever happened to you?

How many times have you been out somewhere, maybe a park or the beach, and your cell phone battery is dying? You aren't going to find an electrical socket buried in the sand or attached to a tree. So, all you have to do is pull out your solar charger and let the sun take care of the rest. Check out solar chargers at www.livesmartinfo.com/solarchargers to see what Amazon has.

You could also use a manual, hand-crank charger. There are actually LED flashlights powered by hand-cranking. Take a look at some here: www.livesmartinfo.com/handcrankchargers, from Amazon as well. Turning the crank for 1 minute will power the flashlight for an entire hour! And when the light goes out, you don't have to worry about finding new batteries; all you need to do is turn the crank again and the light will turn back on. This is especially useful during blackouts and camping trips.

3. What About Batteries?

Batteries come in a variety of shapes and sizes. It can power anything from your wristwatch to your car. Considering how much we depend on batteries, it should be no surprise that at least 15 billion batteries are produced globally every year. Out of that 15 billion, the United States purchases nearly 3 billion. And out of that 3 billion, nearly 179,000 tons of batteries end up in landfills across the country every year.

You may think "big deal, they're just batteries." Well, actually, it is a big deal. The manufacturing of batteries alone consumes a lot of resources and usually also involves hazardous chemicals. For further details, (visit http://www.myecomaid.com/2011/12/everything-you-need-to-know-to-be-green-with-your-electronics-and-becoming-more-eco-friendly/. Some of the elements that make up batteries today are cadmium, lead, and mercury (although mercury has been banned in most cases). Now imagine 179,000 tons of batteries slowly breaking down in a landfill. Those chemicals will leak out of the batteries and into the environment. Once in the environment, they can poison the land, the animals, and even your water supply. Enough exposure to all that toxicity may give you a whole mess of health problems, like high blood pressure, dementia, or it could simply kill you.

Go "rechargeable" Green

Get yourself a battery charger and rechargeable batteries. Go to www.livesmartinfo.com/batterycharger and see what they have on Amazon. They can be reused again and again and again, keeping more money in your pocket and more batteries out of landfills. Plus, 1 billion kilowatt hours of power could be saved every year (in the US), if people used energy efficient battery chargers. This would also save more than $100 million each year and prevent more than 1 million tons of greenhouse gases from being released into the atmosphere.

If you do have to buy non-rechargeable batteries, go for the Lithium-Ion (Li-Ion) and Nickel Metal Hydride (NiMH) batteries. Li-Ion batteries are a bit more expensive; but they come with a higher energy/weight ration, higher voltage, and will hold their charge for a longer period of time when not in use.

Regardless of which type of battery you use, when it comes time to dispose of them, **do not throw your batteries in the trash;** recycle them! BatteryRecycling.com and Call2Recycle.org offer battery recycling programs for individuals, businesses, and corporations. Also, search Earth911.com to see where you can recycle batteries in your local area.

Benefits of eCycling

- Ecycled products get turned into new electronics thus putting these valuable materials back to good use and avoid drawing further on the earth's natural resources.
- Many companies these days are using parts from recycled electronics to make new cell phones, laptops, and more; which is far more beneficial for the environment than throwing them in the trash.
- Safely recycling and reusing electronics helps keep substances like lead and mercury from harming people or the environment.
- Recycling and reusing electronics creates jobs for professional recyclers and refurbishers. It also creates new markets for the valuable components that are dismantled.
- For further related details, definitely visit http://www.myecomaid.com/2011/12/everything-you-need-to-know-to-be-green-with-your-electronics-and-becoming-more-eco-friendly/.

Recycling CFLs (Compact Fluorescent Light Bulb) - What You Need To Know!

While we're on the subject of recycling, I thought it was important to mention CFLs - you know - the swirly bulb. I call it "early 21st century lighting" because it's replacing the traditional incandescent bulbs (which is steadily on its way out) that we've been accustomed to using during the last century. The good thing is that it uses less energy to provide the same amount of lighting which saves money on your energy bill. But they do cost a little more than the other bulb type.

If you're not sure how much light one bulb provides, think of "lumens" (or "lm") for brightness instead of watts (the old way). For example, a 100w incandescent bulb = a 1600lm CFL. Here's a handy chart:

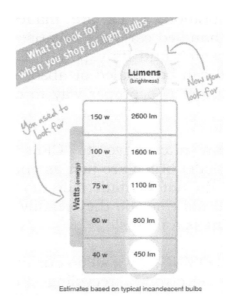

What to look for when you shop for light bulbs

Now you look for

You used to look for

Lumens (brightness)

Watts (energy)	Lumens (brightness)
150 w	2600 lm
100 w	1600 lm
75 w	1100 lm
60 w	800 lm
40 w	450 lm

Estimates based on typical incandescent bulbs

On the package there should be a Lighting Facts label that provides details about the bulb for its brightness, lifespan, and energy used in terms of watts.

CFLs do have a dark side that you should be aware of.

They contain mercury (aka "quicksilver") within its glass tubing which is a heavy, silvery transition metal that is toxic to your health and to the environment when it ends up in landfills thus contributing to air and groundwater pollution. This is why they need to be recycled instead of just disposing into the trash bin.

The Environmental Protection Agency ("EPA") has a website that you can check out to see if there are any CFL collection opportunities in your area. Find out by visiting this link: http://www.epa.gov/cfl/cflrecycling.html or this one: www.earth911.com.

In addition, CFLs are made of glass and should be handled carefully because if dropped and it breaks, watch out! Its vapors quickly escape into the air and can be inhaled or absorbed through the skin. But there is a proper way to clean it up. See the details here: http://www.epa.gov/cfl/cflcleanup.html.

As an alternative to CFLs, LEDs (Light-Emitting Diode) bulbs are just as energy efficient as CFLs and do not contain mercury substance nor toxic chemicals - nor do they readily attract insects, which *I think* is a bonus!

IN CLOSING, if we all do our little part when it comes to electronic recycling ("eCycling") and recycling in general, what a difference that can make in our environment, landfills, and not to mention the peace of mind we'll get knowing that we're doing the right thing. Let's all continue to do our little part for an impact on a larger scale!

NOTE: Harry - "My Eco Guy" - Helped contribute to this Chapter. Visit MyEcoMaid.com for more eco-friendly tips from him.

CHAPTER ~2~

GREEN CLEANING 101 - DIY NATURAL CLEANING SOLUTIONS WITH VINEGAR AND OTHER FRUGAL RESOURCES THAT YOU ALREADY HAVE

Courtesy of Rubbermaid Products

It's a given that popular cleaning products that you buy from the store are full of chemicals which means they are harmful to you, your family and your pets; not to mention the environment. Plus overall they're more expensive. Some of these substances include ammonia, chemically engineered perfumes, chlorine, dyes, phosphates, other solvents and neurotoxins.

Sometimes just opening the container can give you a headache and cause nausea from the toxic fumes.

There's a delicate eco system here. When these chemical cleaning solutions have been used (sometimes all of it doesn't even get used), it's thrown into the trash which ends up in landfills thus polluting the soil and groundwater. This is harmful to living species because it eventually gets into their system.

So we'll take an alternative "natural" route that's safe, effective and have been around way before the 21st century! Most of the items listed below you probably already have in your home somewhere. And what's really nice is that they're affordable for most people. But you will be amazed at what they can do as far as cleaning is concerned.

It's been said that "natural" cleaning solutions are weak when it comes to doing a good cleaning, removing stains, etc. in comparisons to chemical commercial household cleaners. That's sometimes why people tend to shy away from eco-friendly products. If that describes how you feel, simply make your homemade cleaning solution a little more concentrated, and apply a little more manual scrubbing pressure. You'll be pleasantly surprised!

Listed below are 11 items we can use to make up our natural homemade cleaning concoctions and deodorizers for different parts of your home (bathroom, kitchen, bedroom, closet, living room, etc.). Interestingly, each item can be used in various other ways. But to keep it manageable, we will focus on their "cleaning" purposes.

Also, you'll find that some of the solutions overlap. In other words, if there's an ingredient you don't have readily available there might be another ingredient that you do have that can serve the same purpose. Let's break them down and have some fun with this!

1) SALT (aka Sodium Chloride)

(Most likely already have it at home or can buy it anywhere)

Salt is most commonly used as a food enhancer. But there's so much more to what it can be used for; especially for cleaning. It can be added with other natural cleaning ingredients or used alone to handle certain tasks.

5 Ways to use it for cleaning purposes

1. For removing coffee and tea stains from cups - dampen a cloth and sprinkle salt onto it and rub in circular motions.

2. As an ant deterrent - Make an unbroken path of salt across window frames and doorways. They wouldn't dare cross it! This might work for other little bugs too. Try it.

3. For polishing copper and silver - Make a thick paste with salt and vinegar. Apply the paste with a soft cloth onto your items. Then thoroughly rinse and dry them.

4. For removing that dull yellow look from white cotton and linen fabrics after you've had them for a while - boil them in salt and baking soda for an hour

5. For absorbing grease from pans - Sprinkle the grease with salt which absorbs it. Then wipe it. This will make it easier when it's time to wash it.

2) *(WHITE)* VINEGAR (aka Impure Dilute Acetic Acid)

(Can buy it anywhere)

Just by making a 50/50 solution of vinegar and water and putting it in a spray bottle, you'll have a natural, **all-purpose cleaner for countertops, stovetops, appliances, etc.** Vinegar is a primary ingredient for eco-friendly cleaning solutions considering it is a **deodorizer and disinfectant** which you'll see as you continue reading. It **removes soap scum, cleans shower doors and windows, cuts grease, clean linoleum and tile** (in most cases; test a little first).
CAUTION: Do not use vinegar on marble, no-wax floors, stones or hardwood floors (undiluted) as it is acidic.

1. **Use undiluted, pure white vinegar to clean and remove the ring in toilet bowls** - It works best if the water level is lower, so flush the toilet and then pour the vinegar all around the inside of the rim. If you want to thicken it, just sprinkle a little baking soda for extra cleaning power and then start scrubbing.
2. **For laundry** - Vinegar can also be used as a natural fabric softener by adding just a ½-cup in your rinsing cycle.

3) BAKING SODA (aka Sodium Bicarbonate)

(Can buy it anywhere)

This is a mild abrasive and primary ingredient for eco-friendly **multipurpose cleaning**. It can be used as a **deodorizer** all by itself. It can also be used as a **carpet deodorizer, a copper and brass tarnish remover, scouring powder, silver cleaner, marble cleaner**, and many more uses.

1. **For a carpet stain remover** - Form a paste by mixing baking soda and white vinegar together. Use a small brush (maybe a toothbrush) and work the paste into the stain. Vacuum up the baking soda after it's thoroughly dry. Depending on how well it comes out, you might need to repeat this process on the stain.

2. **For cleaning the drain of your sink** - First, pour a ½ cup of baking soda down the drain. Second, pour a ½ cup of white vinegar. Third, for 15 minutes, leave it alone. And fourth, pour 2 quarts of boiling water to wash it down the drain.

4) TEA TREE OIL (aka Melaleuca Alternifolia Oil)

(Can buy it at any drug store in the pharmacy area and health food stores)

5 Ways to use it for cleaning purposes

1. **Use as a shower, tub and tile cleaner.**
2. **Can be used as an antiseptic.**
3. **Add a small amount to laundry to remove musty, lingering odors**
4. **For mold and mildew control** - Simply add 2 teaspoons of tea tree oil to 2 cups of water in a spray bottle. Shake well to blend. Spray your shower walls <u>without</u> rinsing. It usually takes a few days until the smell goes away. Its anti-fungal properties help to control mold and mildew.

If you spray the grout, the must and mold will be killed but the discoloration remains. It's the opposite of bleach in the sense that bleach removes the black mold color; but it doesn't kill the mold, which comes back. The tea tree oil kills the mold.

5. As a general purpose cleaner - Fill a 12 ounce spray bottle with warm distilled water. Add in 1 teaspoon of tea tree oil, 2 tablespoons of distilled white vinegar, and 1 teaspoon of Borax. Mix or shake it up until the Borax is fully dissolved. It also wipes out odor causing bacteria.

5) HYDROGEN PEROXIDE (aka H2o2)

(Can buy it anywhere - the traditional 3% solution is referred to here which is what is commonly sold)

10 Ways to use it for cleaning purposes

1.   All-purpose cleaner for tubs, sinks and countertops - Put a little on your cleaning cloth and wipe or spray the surface to kill germs and leave a refreshing scent.

2. Cleaning wooden cutting boards - Simply pour some on it to kill salmonella and other bacteria.

3. Cleaning toothbrushes - To kill germs, it must be soaked immediately after being poured from the bottle because H2o2 loses potency quickly after being exposed to light. No wonder it's packaged in dark bottles! Rinse it well before using your toothbrush again.

4. For a toilet or septic system disinfectant - In a dark spray bottle that filters out sunlight, fill a half with hydrogen peroxide and the other half with water. Spray some on the inside of the toilet bowl and let it stay for at least a few minutes then you can use a scrub brush to clean it. Your septic will not be damaged because the H2o2 will be diluted by the time you flush it. This is a great alternative instead of using bleach.

5.   For whitening laundry - Instead of using bleach, add 1 cup of H2o2 to a load of laundry. Specifically to get blood out of the fabric, pour some directly on the spot and let it presoak for about 1 minute. Then rub that area and rinse with cold water. You can repeat the process if needed. Do not overdo it unless you want to ruin your fabric as H2o2 is a bleaching agent!

6. For mopping floors - Pour 1 gallon of hot water in a bucket along with a ½ cup of hydrogen peroxide.

7.   For cleaning mold and mildew - In a dark spray bottle that filters out sunlight, fill 2/3 of it with water and the remaining 1/3 with H2o2. Spray the affected area and let it stay for a minimum of 10 minutes then wipe it off. In general, considering it's a bleaching agent, be mindful of what you use it on to preserve the colors of things.

8.   For cleaner dishes - If you're hand washing, add a ½ cup to your sink's dish water.

9.   For a fruit and vegetable wash - In a dark spray bottle that filters out sunlight, fill it with half water and half H2o2. Spray it thoroughly to kill bacteria and neutralize chemicals (especially if it was sprayed with pesticides which mean anything that's not organic) and rinse. To add longevity to your produce, do this right away when you get home.

10. For cleaning bacteria out of sponges - Pour half water and half hydrogen peroxide in a shallow dish. Soak the sponge in it for 10 minutes. Then thoroughly rinse it out and let it completely dry before the next use.

6) BORAX (aka Sodium Borate)

(Can buy it at hardware stores, some supermarkets, international grocery stores, or online. Commonly sold under the name "**20 Mule Team**")

12 Ways it can be used

1. It has anti-microbial properties and can be used as a **disinfectant**. (There's no smell either.)

2. Inhibits molds and fungal growth

3. When combined with other cleaning products, it **enhances the cleaning power**.

4. Used for **cleaning carpet**; (but that's not the best time to have crawling babies and pets around)

5. Can be used to clean surfaces, including chopping boards - But wear gloves and rinse well when cleaning because it's strongly alkaline

6. Kills cockroaches, ants, fleas and other little insects; so don't inhale it!

7. Good deterrent for mice as they get bent out of shape when it touches their feet

8. For sinks and drains - Simply combine it with hot water

9. For getting rid of grease - Just add it to water along with liquid dish washing solution; rinse well

10. For cleaning windows, enamel surfaces and tiles - Add 1 tablespoon or a bit more to 2 or 3 liters of hot water depending on how grimy they are.

11. For cleaning ovens - Combine Borax, vinegar and baking soda into a paste. Take a brush to apply it throughout the oven. Let it sit there for at least several hours. Finally take a damp cloth to wipe it all off. Doing it this way totally spares you from those highly toxic commercial oven cleaners.

12. For boosting laundry detergent - Add a ½ cup to each wash load to remove soap residue from clothing, neutralize laundry odors, soften hard water, whiten whites and increase laundry detergents stain removal ability.

CAUTION: Don't mix it with or store it with acids. Keep it away from kids and pets.

You can take a look at Amazon to see Borax in its many forms here: www.livesmartinfo.com/boraxproducts.

7) LEMONS / LEMON JUICE / LEMON ESSENTIAL OIL

(Can buy at the grocery store)

7 ways to use it for cleaning purposes

1. Use as a **disinfectant**
2. **Use to remove grease stains and mineral build-up** because of its acidity
3. Used as a **bleaching agent**
4. **For an all-purpose, naturally scented cleaner -** Combine the following into a spray bottle and shake it up: 3½ cups of hot water, ¼ cup of white vinegar, ¼ cup of dishwashing liquid, 2 teaspoons of Borax, and at least 6 drops of lemon essential oil.
5. **For deodorizing and cleaning garbage disposal** - Cut the peel off a lemon (or an orange peel can do the job too). Put it in the drain of your garbage disposal and let it run for 3 minutes. You'll be left with a fresh smell because it'll kill odor-causing bacteria and dissolve food build up.
6. **For wood furniture polish** - First wipe the furniture with a cloth to remove any excessive dust. In a spray bottle, combine a half cup of lemon juice with one cup of olive oil. Shake it up so that they blend together. Then spray a little on a cloth and rub the furniture with it. Use a separate dry cloth to wipe it dry.

7. For removing rust - Make a paste with 50/50 lemon juice and Borax. Apply it directly onto the rust or submerge it into the solution. Let it sit for 25 to 30 minutes. Then use a damp cloth to wipe it off. But if you rinse it off, make sure to thoroughly dry it. You might need to do this process twice if you still see rust. Don't overdo it because you don't want to eat away the outer metal coating which would expose the underlying dull base metal.

8) RAW POTATOES

(Can buy at the grocery store)

How to use it for cleaning purposes

Remove rust from your cast iron cookware, baking pans, knives or other tools - Cut a russet or red potato either across in half or lengthwise, or just enough to where you can comfortably grip it. Dip the cut end in salt or baking soda and scrub the rusted area. If it gets slippery, thinly cut off the already used surface of the potato and repeat the same thing until the rust is gone. Then rinse and dry off.

9) BAMBOO CHARCOAL DEODORIZER (aka Activated Carbon)

(Can buy it online)

What it is used for

It's extremely porous and can be used as a general **deodorizer to absorb moister, smells and lingering or foul odors** in refrigerators, freezers, closets, drawers, cupboards, shoe areas, under the kitchen sink, bathrooms; litter boxes, just about anywhere; including your car. It's non-toxic and environmentally safe. Some prefer it over baking soda.

What forms it comes in

The size, shape and containers of it depend on where you want to place it to refresh the air. For example, the **bamboo charcoal deodorizer** comes in a pouch and there are different pouch sizes. It is the most popular. There's a **powder** kind that can be turned into a thick cleaning agent and also a **mud that can deodorize toilet bowls** up to 6 months. This is definitely worth looking into further as not enough people are aware of how wonderful this is. If you would like to see the various forms it's packaged in at Amazon, take a look here: www.livesmartinfo.com/bamboocharcoaldeodorizers .

10) RUBBING ALCOHOL (aka Isopropyl Alcohol)

(Flammable and not to drink - Can buy it anywhere)

12 ways to use it for cleaning purposes

1. For Cleaning chrome - Take a soft, absorbent cloth and pour some rubbing alcohol onto it. Wipe the chrome and no rinsing is necessary. It'll kill the germs and evaporate.

2. Cleaning venetian blind slats - Get a flat tool such as a 6-inch drywall knife or spatula and wrap it in cloth. Put a rubber band around it to secure it.

Simply dip it in rubbing alcohol and start cleaning away.

3. To prevent window frosting during winter - Wash your windows with one quart of water and a ½ cup of rubbing alcohol. After washing, use newspaper to polish it for a shine.

4. To remove hair spray from mirrors - Those hair spray spots are stubborn! Clean your mirrors with rubbing alcohol and it'll remove the sticky residue.

5. Getting rid of fruit flies - Fill a spray bottle with rubbing alcohol. As the annoying little gnats are flying around, spray them to drop dead. It's not as strong as a commercial insecticide; but it's more eco-friendly.

6. Removing ink stains - Presoak the spot(s) for a few minutes in rubbing alcohol just before laundering.

7. For preventing neck stain around the collar - Wipe your neck with rubbing alcohol before getting dressed and it'll help prevent that ring around the collar of your clothing.

8. For cleaning the phone - Wipe your phone down with rubbing alcohol to both disinfect it and cut through the grime.

9. To remove permanent marker stains from countertops - Most countertops are made from non-permeable material such as plastic laminate or perhaps marble. Use rubbing alcohol to dissolve marker stains back to a liquid state and then simply wipe it off.

10. For removing dog ticks - Dab the leech with rubbing alcohol which causes it to loosen its grip. Then grab it as close to the dog's skin as possible to pull it straight out. To disinfect that area, simply dab it again with rubbing alcohol.

11. For dissolving windshield frost - Fill a spray bottle with rubbing alcohol and spray the car glass. Instead of scraping, simply wipe the frost off easily.

11) OLIVE OIL

(Can buy at the grocery store)

5 ways to use it for cleaning purposes

1. To help prevent wicker furniture from cracking - Use a soft cloth to gently rub the oil into it. Warming the olive oil works better.

2. Remove scratches from leather (furniture, jackets, etc.) - Pour just a dab onto a cotton cleaning cloth and in a circular motion lightly rub it into the scratch.

3. Get paint off your hands - Rub some into your skin where the paint is and leave it there for 5 minutes then thoroughly wash your hands with soap.

4. Use as a door hinge lubrication - Gets rid of the squealing sound.

5. For polishing wood furniture - Mix together 2 cups of olive oil and 1 cup of either lemon juice or vinegar. Dip a soft cloth into the solution and rub it into the furniture. To get out scratches, make the solution 50/50 which means if you use 1 cup of olive oil, also use 1 cup of either lemon juice or vinegar. Combine them together and rub out the scratch.

8 Helpful Cleaning Aids

1. Spray bottle - Keep in mind not to reuse spray bottles that have contained other chemicals.

2.   Squeegee - A great tool to use when cleaning windows.

3.   Cleaning rag or cloth - There's no need to go out and buy this. Just use an old piece of 100% cotton clothing that you no longer wear; but cut out the zipper or cut off the buttons. You can even use old towels or worn out bed sheets which you can cut into different sizes if you want.

4.   Natural sponges - Great for cleaning stains off carpets.

5.   Microfiber cloth - Its fibers are made of nylon and polyester that's finely split and woven into soft, absorbent, and thin material. Because it is electrostatic, dust naturally attracts to it. The fibers absorbs dirt and oil and does not shed lint like other cloths and paper towels; which makes it easier to clean mirrors with no streaking either. Interestingly, it can repel water; yet when dampened with hot water, it's great for cleaning window frames, walls and countertops without cleaning solution. They cost a little more but last longer because you can wash and reuse them. And they dry really fast too. You should be able to find these around at drugstores or car accessories stores. But you can definitely find them online. If you want to see what they look like, you can see it at Amazon here: www.livesmartinfo.com/microfibercloth.

6.   Scrub brush (soft and firm bristles) - Some brush bristles are firmer for hard scrubbing that doesn't damage the article. But soft bristles are for more delicate items that still need a scrub. You can also use a toothbrush if that's more suitable for what you are cleaning.

7.   Razorblade - Makes it easy to scrape off dried and stuck-on things from mirrors.

8.   Newspaper - Instead of paper towels, newspapers are great for wiping windows and mirrors.

Granted, some people are not into measuring things and mixing cleaning solutions. That's fine. This is where you can alternatively go to the health food store, hardware store, grocery store or online and buy "natural" cleaning products that's already mixed with these same natural ingredients. These are becoming more available now because companies are feeling the pressure to become more eco-friendly, safer and less toxic.

It's nice to know there are so many other less costly options available for cleaning that we can all take advantage of and thus contribute to a safer environment for the planet.

RESOURCES:

- http://chemistry.about.com/od/chemicaldata bases/a/Chemical-Names-Of-Common-Substances.htm
- http://chemistry.about.com/od/howthingswo rkfaqs/a/howboraxworks.htm
- http://www.greenfootsteps.com/borax-information.html#anchor-name
- http://www.teatreewonders.com/household-cleaning-products.html#
- http://www.truthorfiction.com/rumors/h/hy drogen-peroxide.htm

- http://www.ecologycenter.org/factsheets/cleaning.html
- http://en.wikipedia.org/wiki/Activated_carbon
- http://www.dailygrommet.com/products/253-ever-bamboo-charcoal-deodorizer-for-closets-shoes-rooms-all-natural

CHAPTER ~3~

ORGANIC GARDENING 101 - "HOW TO" ESSENTIALS AND TIPS FOR STARTING AN OUTDOOR OR INDOOR ORGANIC VEGETABLE GARDEN

Courtesy of Lamiot

It is not a passing trend that the demand for organic produce remains on the rise. Although you are being charged at least a third more for it than the cost of non-organic produce, it continues to be in demand for health reasons and avoidance of pesticides and synthetic fertilizers.

With the economy affecting spending money these days, it's not uncommon to see someone give up buying something else just to make sure they have enough money for their organic vegetables and fruits. If you are a vegetarian or are health-conscious, buying fresh organic vegetables and fruits can take a bite out of your wallet.

That's one of the reasons why more people are turning to organic gardening whether that's at their local nursery, in their apartment if they don't have access to land, or usually in their backyard if they live in a house. But despite what has gotten you interested in organic gardening, it's certainly doable and we're going to cover some of the essentials to get you started.

What Is Organic Gardening?

Organic gardening means to raise vegetables, fruits, herbs (whatever you enjoy) without using growth regulators such as pesticides, chemical fertilizers and fungicides. Instead, minerals and germs that are non-synthetic like earth worms, algae, fungi, bacteria, natural biological cycles, compost, manures and composting techniques are used. These are vital in growing natural plants with nothing artificial to making a "sustainable" garden.

If you don't know much about gardening at all or if you're new to organic gardening, there's terminology that you should be familiar with because these are things you're going to be using. Some of the terms might sound shocking initially, but you'll get over it. Here they are:

1) Compost is natural or organic waste (manure) used as plant fertilizer. It's composed of fruit and vegetable peels, rejected or rotten produce, dried grass clippings, crushed eggshells, leaves, crop residue, shredded paper, old sod, tea bags, poultry manure, etc. That was just a partial list. You can easily make up this concoction yourself all year long and put it in your "compost" container so that you'll have enough to use because as these materials decay or decompose, it'll compact and turn into humus (dark, rich matter that boosts fertility and enriches soil) and won't be as "big" as when you began collecting it.

You can tell when compost is ready to be used because it will no longer give off decomposing steam and the color will be both dark and crumbly, which on the average takes about +/- 8 months. So if you want to take this natural route for your organic garden, you'd better get started!

You'll most likely need a **compost bin** and there are many different types. For example, if you live in an apartment, make up a compost of food scraps which would be kept in a countertop composter. There are also larger ones that can be kept in backyards. If you would like to see the different styles of compost bins, check out www.livesmartinfo.com/compostbins to see a wide selection at Amazon. Using compost for your soil is so much healthier and better for the soil because it's so natural which supports the growth of your plants.   If you would like further details about different types of composting, see Resource 1 at the end of this chapter.

If making your own compost doesn't sound exciting, you can buy it from any certified organic source that's reputable like a local nursery or garden center that promotes organic materials.

2)   Mulch is a top layer that's placed over garden soil to keep it enriched and moist so that you don't have to water it as much. It's also a weed deterrent to prevent sprouting. If it's windy or rains, it helps to keep the soil from eroding because of its thickness as well as keeping the soil temperature moderate for better growth.

There are different things you can use to make up mulch which includes chopped tree bark, hay, wood shavings, pine needles, sawdust, twigs, crushed peanut shells, etc. It's used as more of a soil protector rather than compost and it can look relatively decorative too.

3) Blood Meal is powdered or dried animal blood from cows or other animals from slaughterhouses. It speeds up decomposition in compost piles because of its concentrated nitrogen level which is a good source of food for garden soil. However, it is important to closely follow the instructions on the package for applying it to avoid burning your plants to death from the nitrogen.

Something else that adds nitrogen to the soil is to plant legumes or use a certified organic liquid fish emulsion.

4) Bone Meal is animal bones that have been cooked, grounded up and packaged from the meat processing industry. It is a natural, organic slow-release fertilizer that's a good source of phosphorus which assists with seed, cell formation and division, and plant root growth in your soil.

Additional "meals" that promote soil nutrition are cotton seed meal, alfalfa meal and greensand. Also, for phosphorus and essential minerals, ground rock powders can be mixed with soil.

Soil Testing

You must test your soil to make sure it is sustainable and ideal for plant growth. This includes the soils' fertility level, acidity (pH), texture, mineral density, drainage and composition, among other things. Soils can be categorized as **sandy** (doesn't retain moisture and nutrients; quick draining), **claylike** (slow draining; but nutrient rich) or **loamy (or fertile)** which is suitable because it's not soggy and retains nutrients and moisture.

How to manually test your soil - To figure out what type of soil you have, simply take a handful of moist soil (it should not be wet) from the area where you want to plant your garden, and firmly squeeze it. Afterward, open your hand and look for these 3 signs: (1) Sandy soil = it fell apart as soon as you opened your hand. (2) Clay soil = when poked, it continues to keep its shape. (3) Loamy soil = it holds its shape; but when lightly poked, it crumbles nicely.

Soil testing kit - If you prefer, alternatively you can use an electronic soil tester or soil testing kit which gives a quick and accurate reading of what your soil consists of and is very easy to use. There are many types to choose from and you can see the selection Amazon has at www.livesmartinfo.com/soiltestingkits.

Using either method, once you know what type of soil you have, you'll be able to tell what it needs for plant selection, level of fertility and overall preparation.

9 Tools to Assist You with Gardening (find at any hardware store)

1. **Gloves** - Protecting your hands with gloves is a good idea; especially if you're working with compost.

2. **Shovel** - Great for scooping large amounts of soil.

3. **Gardening Fork (or Tine Fork)** - It has 4 strong steel prongs (or spikes) that push easily into the ground to loosen and turn over soil. There are

short ones too with a wooden handle and the tines are closer together for light weeding.

4. Hand Trowel - A pointed, scoop-shaped metal blade that's great for breaking up soil and digging small holes for transferring plants to pots, mixing in fertilizer, planting and weeding.

5. Gardening Spade - It has a metal tip for digging and its shape allows for soil transferring. It's like a miniature handheld shovel.

6. Grub Hoe - a sharp, vertical flat edged blade (or prying bar) connected to the end of a long wooden pole for digging, weed chopping, piling soil around the base of plants, slicing and shallow trenching for planting seeds. It's also great for getting stones out of the soil ground.

7. Rake - Convenient for heaping leaves or hay.

8. Watering Can - You don't want to drench your garden area with water using a hose. So a watering can filled with water that has a spout and handle is more controllable on the soil and delicate plants.

9. (OPTIONAL) Water/Rain Butt (Rain Barrel) - This is a great backup for basic sustainability. Simply place it underneath any residential gutter spout so that when it rains, instead of the rainwater going to waste in storm drains, it can run off from your rooftop and collect straight into the mouth of the rain barrel. And it's natural "soft water" without chlorine, lime or calcium. For purposes of your garden, it's good to have one of these for spare water just in case your area is having a drought and you don't want your vegetable garden to dry up. You can see examples of rain barrels on Amazon at www.livesmartinfo.com/rainbarrels

Why Begin With Organic Seeds

Although it's easier to just purchase plant seedlings (a young or baby plant) and grow them to maturity, when you are building an organic garden there are benefits for using organic seeds from the very beginning including better control over the products you'll be using for it.

You do want to make sure that your seeds are one hundred percent certified organic seeds that are harvested from plants with no fungicides, pesticides, synthetic chemical fertilizers and no residues from such chemicals. They need to be pure or completely adapted to sustainable organic growing practices. You will see and taste the difference when it reaches maturity. Buy your seeds early in the season.

Aside from a greater variety of vegetable seeds that you might not be able to get as seedlings anyway, some nurseries or garden centers do spray non-organic products onto their seedlings to keep unwanted critters away and as an instant nutrient booster. In addition, nurseries have a more conducive environment with specialized greenhouses that provide ideal conditions for seeds to develop in. So once you bring the seedlings home to a harsh environment, they might not adapt as well and have more of a struggle to grow in totally organic fertilizers from chemical ones that they've already been used to. Plus it's a more satisfying experience to grow your vegetables from the actual seeds. Just keep the seed packets and follow the directions on how to take care of them the proper way. Get them before they expire and keep the last frost date in mind for your area which is the last spring day that there might be a killing frost.

How to Plant Your Seeds (Outdoors)

Courtesy of OakleyOriginals

Your organic garden bed (or soil) must be prepared before sowing seeds. This is done by using the appropriate tools mentioned earlier as well as testing the soil for fertility. Choose a location where there is never standing water. Remove any grass by slicing out the sod and shaking off as much soil as possible. Also remove any large, hard lumps and rocks so that the tender roots of your developing plant can penetrate through without nutrients being blocked.

You can till the soil to around 12 inches deep using a grub hoe. The appropriate compost to put into your soil so that your seeds have a healthy place to start will depend on your soil analysis and which vegetable seeds you are going to plant. Be sure to include garlic, marigold flowers and onions as organic garden pests can't stand them!

When planting seeds, be careful not to place them deep into the soil as that will suffocate them. Less than 1 inch deep is sufficient; but if the seeds are very tiny they'll grow better just being left on top of the soil. Give emerging plants room to grow by not overcrowding the seeds. Keep the soil's surface evenly moist, perhaps with a little mulch soon after planting, but do not soak the seeds in water or else they will rot. Just a light sprinkle will keep the soil from drying out if planted during summer's peak.

If you're in an area where it's windy or cold, it's okay to cover your vegetables with a cloche as that really does help to shield some of the harshness.

Are Wild Animals and Pests Trying To Freeload? Fight Back - Naturally!

Depending on the location of your garden and other factors, you will have uninvited company to your vegetable garden. They're going to know what you're up to and try to sabotage it. But you can stop them! **Here are 8 things that you can try:**

1. Put a tall wire mesh fence around your garden.

2. On the outskirts of your vegetable garden, **plant garlic and onions** which they're just not into.

3. Companion planting means to plant pungent herbs (like dill, rosemary, etc.) along with specific flowers such as daisies, bee-balm and lavender to deter pests.

4. On tomato stems, wrap an **aluminum foil collar band**.

5. To remove pests from leaves, use masking tape to get them off easier and they'll get stuck to it.

6. Spray your plant branches with **insecticidal soaps** which is a safe solvent made from naturally occurring plant oils formulated with fatty acids that kill the "bad" insects; not the beneficial ones like praying mantis, ladybugs, etc. This is not commercial dishwashing soap that you use for washing dishes. It's more effective if sprayed in the early morning or late evening when the drops will take longer to evaporate because the bugs have to make direct contact with it. *(See Resource #1)*

7. Diatomaceous Earth is a lethal dust with microscopic razor sharp edges which comes from shells of tiny critters called diatoms. The insects eat this dust and get their insides shredded. It's nonpoisonous, safe for both humans and animals, and is ecologically safe. It kills snails, slugs, all kinds of flies and a slew of other little critters. However, it doesn't discriminate; ALL bugs will get cut, so be discriminant. But it's safe for your garden. *(See Resource #2)*

8. **Bacillus thuringiensis (Bt)-based (Kurstaki strain)** is a natural occurring bacterial disease of insects which are the active ingredient in some insecticides. It kills leaf and needle-feeding caterpillars, but they have to eat it first. It's nontoxic to people, pets and wildlife. *(See Resource #3)*

How to Create an "Indoor" Organic Garden for Fresh Vegetables and Herbs

Courtesy of Hair Squared

Indoor gardening within various containers is the next best thing if you don't have access to an outdoor garden; especially if you live in an apartment with limited space. Plus you will have more control over heat, water and light. It's certainly better if you have a balcony or patio. But if not, as long as you have a windowsill it can strategically be done.

How is your indoor lighting? Indoor vegetable gardening requires very good lighting. Any south-facing window is ideal; but a constant 6 hours of sunlight in any indoor area will be fine. Supplemental artificial lighting such as a fluorescent "grow light" along with natural light is also helpful for promoting a healthy garden. It's best to group together plants with similar needs.

Dwarf or Miniature Varieties of Vegetables

Dwarf or miniature varieties of vegetables are being developed more and more which takes up less space and doesn't take as long to grow. This is conducive to indoor gardening. You can check with larger organic seed companies to see what's available. In the meantime, some of the more common vegetables and cooking herbs that grow well indoors are:

- **Leafy salad greens** such as leaf lettuce, spinach, miniature cabbages and radish are easy to grow in light to partially shaded areas and doesn't require as much space. A miniature variety of head lettuce such as Tom Thumb that you can plant grows pretty fast as well as Bloomsdale spinach which you can plant every few weeks for a convenient ongoing supply.

- **Mushrooms** don't require much maintenance and prefer to grow in darker places like attics and even cupboards. It's very simple to grow as an indoor vegetable.

- **Miniature carrots** is a root vegetable that's great for indoor container gardening and doesn't need deep soil to grow and does fine in partial sunlight. Little Finger is one of the miniature varieties that you can plant.

- **Cherry tomatoes** are the best kind of tomatoes for an indoor garden. Ideally, an upside down planter (with a hole in the bottom) that suspends from the ceiling thus allowing the plant to grow downward works great. You've probably seen those before. But if that's not feasible in your living space, you can use a larger pot which holds more soil and moisture. But for better results, put a bamboo cane stake in the soil so that the stalk does not bend when the tomatoes start to bear. There are a variety of cherry tomatoes that you can plant including Sweet 100 Patio, Tiny Tim, Pixie and Small Fry. However, they do require much light and warmth.

- **Beans** are another variety of vegetable that does well indoors. Use hanging pots for beans as this allows their vines to drape over the pot's sides as it grows downward. They should be hung near a window to catch the morning or evening light.

- **Cooking Herbs** such as parsley, sage, chives, thyme, cilantro, oregano, etc. are great for growing indoors. The soil needs to be kept warm and moist for proper germination. The leaves will be lighter in color and grow smaller if it does not get enough light. Do clip them often to stimulate robust growth and use those clippings in your food.

- **Peppers** that are thin, as opposed to thick bell peppers, grow nicely indoors. A couple of the hot ones are Tiny Thai and Cayenne. And a couple mild, sweet pepper flavors are Yolo Wonder and Sweet Banana. Use them fresh or dried.

The list above is just a partial list of vegetables that can be grown indoors. There are so many others not mentioned here.

What Containers to Use and How to Grow Seeds - "Indoors"

You want to make sure any container that you use has a lot of space so that the roots can comfortably grow. However, it's best to use containers that are designated for plant use as some are deeper or wider depending on the type of plant it's being used for. This means it will have sufficient drainage and will be large enough to host both seedlings and mature plants of its type. So the type of vegetable you are planting determines the correct pot size or seeding tray. The seed package will tell you what that is or if you are buying one from a nursery or garden center, someone there would or should know.

If you don't have access to the correct planter, you can temporarily use a milk carton, paper cup, egg carton, or a tin can. It must have drainage holes at the bottom though. But don't use clay pots because they're more apt to drying out quicker than metal, ceramic, plastic or wooden containers. It's really best to use the recommended container for the specific plant.

When growing seeds from a container, you'll need a mixture of organic potting soil and organic fertilizers which you can get from your local gardening center or nursery. You don't want the fertilizers to burn the emerging young root so make sure it's mild enough. Use warm water to moisten the mixture and then place it inside the container. After it has cooled down, look at your seed packet to see how deep you should plant the seeds. If for some reason you don't have the seed packet anymore, as a rule of thumb, press the seed either 2 times its length or a maximum of 4 times its diameter (or span).

Until they germinate, they should be kept away from direct sunlight; but in a warm temperature. You can optionally cover the container but don't forget to regularly check up on it. Unless it has dried out before germination, it shouldn't need any more water because you've already moistened it.

Once they have germinated, place them in your windowsill or a sunny, brighter area to get used to its new surroundings and avoid transfer shock. After you see 2 to 4 leaves, give them some more mild organic fertilizers which will stimulate healthy and fast growth. But don't overdo it because fertilizer buildup is a known problem in plant containers.

The roots will tell you when they are ready to be transplanted because it'll almost fill the container but haven't grown out of the drainage holes yet. It's really a neat process to watch.

7 Helpful Things for Growing Vegetables Indoors To Keep In Mind

1. For temperature control, open or close your blinds

2. Group like plants together

3. High humidity and moderate temperatures are necessary.

4. Be careful to protect plants from drafts

5. To avoid rotting roots because of insufficient drainage, put gravel in a dish and place it underneath the plant container. Doing this provides improved humidity as the water is evaporating from the dish.

6. Plants that grow in containers require more watering because they tend to dry out more.

7. Do not overuse fertilizers

Picking fresh vegetables and herbs when you want to without having to leave your home is awesome! If you are considering an indoor organic vegetable garden, go for it!

IN CLOSING, whether outdoor or indoor organic vegetable gardening is your desire, the information in this chapter should give you an excellent start even if you are a novice! When you visit a garden center or a nursery, don't hold back on asking questions related to the specific plant you are growing. Gardening (or farming) is such a natural thing going all the way back to the first humans. The difference now is that we have to contend with so many chemicals, pesticides and genetic interference of different fruits and vegetables. The innocence of it all has been overtaken to the point where people desire to go back to the natural basics, which is organic gardening.

RESOURCES

1. http://www.weekendgardener.net/organic-pesticide/insecticidal-soap-060706.htm

2. http://www.internet-grocer.net/diatome.htm also http://www.ghorganics.com/DiatomaceousEarth.html

3. http://www.ext.colostate.edu/pubs/insect/05556.html

C H A P T E R ~4~

GREEN FEMININE HYGIENE - SUSTAINABLE FEMALE ALTERNATIVES

Courtesy of mikebaird

Considering this book is about green living, it would not be complete without mention of eco-friendly alternatives for women; especially female teenagers as this gets them off to a good routine right from the start of their menstrual cycle.

This subject is not openly discussed very often. One of the reasons could be because people are not aware that these sustainable alternatives are available and this might be the first time hearing about them. And another could be that large companies producing disposable feminine hygiene products are extremely profitable and would like to remain that way; so they don't draw attention to eco-alternatives.

I think this book will get into the hands of more people "in general" than if I omitted this chapter and wrote a separate book for women. I'm a female and wasn't aware of these alternatives so there's no telling how many others are out there like me that didn't know about these options and would appreciate that it's being mentioned.

With the fast pace of today's world, we live in a "disposable" society - use it once then throw it out. How convenient for living in the western world as I like to call it. Did you know that in under developed countries girls don't go to school and women don't go to work during the days they're on their period? They can't afford disposable feminine hygiene products nor would their town's waste removal system (if they have one) be able to tolerate that burden. When it comes to environmentally-sustainable alternatives, women have choices. Whichever one you think will work better for you, go for it! Let's explore some of them now.

Reusable Menstrual Cup (Also Called Period Cup) - A Green Alternative for Tampons

Most disposable tampons are made of cotton and rayon, which contains small amounts of dioxin (a toxic byproduct) in its fiber during processing. You can read more about this at the following FDA government website: http://www.fda.gov/MedicalDevices/Safety/AlertsandNotices/PatientAlerts/ucm070003.htm

As convenient as it is, flushing tampons down the toilet can clog up plumbing and septic tanks, even the ones that are labeled "flushable". The materials don't break up as well as natural waste. It can even find its way into the ocean, bypassing sewage treatment.

As an eco-friendly alternative, reusable (or washable) menstrual cups are flexible, bell-shaped cups made from latex-free hypoallergenic silicone that collects or stores instead of absorbs menstrual flow. When put in correctly, there's no leakage and it's easy to remove. Just read the directions that come with the brand that you're using. They can last for around a decade! Just think of all the money that'll save you over the years from not buying disposable tampons.

They can be worn up to 12 hours at a time before emptying, and can hold up to twice the amount of fluid as a regular tampon. This is convenient for overnight or any time; especially for women with highly active lifestyles because of sports, travel, etc. Some are one size fits most or there are different sizes depending on the brand.

As far as cleaning a "reusable" menstrual cup, it's easy. Simply rinse and reinsert between each use. Or you can set aside a designated pot for boiling it in water. Some manufacturers sell hypo-allergenic cleaning solutions specifically made for washable menstrual cups that you can use as well.

There are further details and questions that you're probably wondering about. So under resources at the bottom of this chapter I've listed several websites filled with related information that you'll find interesting. You can check out what they look like on Amazon here: www.livesmartinfo.com/reusablemenstrualcups.

Washable/Reusable Cloth Menstrual Pads - A Green Alternative for Disposable Sanitary Napkins

Cloth menstrual pads have been around for quite some time; even before the last century so they are not new. But when disposable sanitary napkins came on the scene, which was very convenient, the cloth ones kind of went by the wayside for the most part. Unfortunately this convenience has brought along with it processed, chlorine bleached, and unnatural materials in order to manufacture it.

Have you ever wondered how over time, disposable sanitary pads have become even thinner but still absorbent? Well, Wikipedia answers it like this: "The absorbent core, made from chlorine bleached wood pulp, could be reduced to make slimmer products with the addition of polyacrylate gels which sucks up the liquid quickly and holds it in a suspension under pressure. The remaining materials are mostly derived from the petroleum industry. The cover stock used is polypropylene non-woven, with the leak-proof barrier made from polyethylene film." - http://en.wikipedia.org/wiki/Sanitary_napkin.

Basically, these materials are not friendly for our bodies or the environment because they contain plastic and are not biodegradable. An astonishing number of used pads go into landfills each year. I do want to mention that in some poor countries, women use newspapers (if they can find any) or tree bark for their makeshift sanitary napkins, which can cause infections. It's incredibly sad how they have to deal with this each month because they don't have access to very much; even to take care of such a natural thing that most just take for granted.

But due to keen awareness of the environmental impact and concern for health, the tide has been steadily reversing to go back to reusable cloth menstrual pads and is picking up momentum now in the 21st century. But unlike in the past, they're a little more modernized, comfortable and colorful!

Varieties and Styles

You can get them in different varieties and customize them including pocket-style or envelope-style which has absorbent layers that can be inserted inside the pad as needed, or inserts-on-top which allows you to fasten the absorbent layers as needed on the top using a button or snap, or the foldable-style allows the pad to fold around the absorbent layers. There's even all-in-ones where the absorbent layer is actually sewn inside the pad. For extra protection you can include a safe Polyurethane Laminate ("PUL") waterproof lining. They're not bulky either; they're actually thinner than you might think and you can get them in 100% organic cotton. They are very smooth and last for quite a few years. Panty liners are available as well. You can check out Amazon to get an idea of what these look like here: www.livesmartinfo.com/reusablesanitarypads

Also take a look at the resources at the end of this chapter. It's not available in all of them as yet; but you should be able to find these reusable alternatives in health food stores. Perhaps you can give them a call first and ask if they carry these items before making a trip specifically for it.

Unlike disposable sanitary napkins, you do need to wash these reusable pads. As with anything else, once you get into a groove with these, it won't be a big deal. It's just a matter of a "regular" routine once a month that you'll get used to. Think about what it was like for women before the conveniences of today or before washing machines were available which even today everyone does not have access to. Get into a regular routine and remind yourself why you're doing this. There are so many good reasons.

By the way, you would be surprised at how many women out there enjoy making homemade cloth menstrual pads for themselves, their daughters and others. The materials they use are very basic. If that interests you, have a look at these sources:

http://www.biblicalscholarship.net/menses.htm
http://www.tinybirdsorganics.com/organiccotton/clothpads.html
http://www.diapersewing.com/clothpads.htm

People go green to different degrees. If a "green" period is one of the ways you are contributing to an eco-friendly environment and sustainability - way to go!

Think about all the female teenagers and women that you know. Share this information with them because the more this gets out there, the better it'll be for our environment.

I agree that the alternatives mentioned here are not inexpensive initially; but over time you'll not only recuperate your money, but you'll be saving money too. This is part of where that saying comes from about going green and saving money. Give it a shot!

RESOURCES:

Menstrual Cups Options

- http://www.divacup.com/en/home/diva_cup/
- http://www.mooncup.co.uk/
- http://www.lunette.com/au/
- http://www.softcup.com/

Washable Cloth Menstrual Pads

- http://www.sckoon.com/clothmenstrualpads.html
- http://lunapads.com/
- http://www.etsy.com/search_results.php?search_query=reusable+sanitary+napkins&filter[0]=handmade

Additional Types of Reusable Menstrual Products in General

- http://naturalparentsnetwork.com/reusable-menstrual-products/
- http://www.ecomenses.com/

C H A P T E R ~5~

NATURAL BABY PRODUCTS - GREEN SURROUNDINGS FOR YOUR BABY

Courtesy of Kmroselle

In this 21st century, if you live in the "city" part of town, there's probably more hustle and bustle, a faster paced lifestyle and more "stuff" in the air than if you live in a more rural area or the countryside.

You have a new baby now (or you have one in the oven almost ready) and you want to shelter or protect him/her as much as possible from the residual effects of the environment. How can you do this? Well, this chapter is going to cover some practical ways to give your baby a more "green" nest, if you will.

The things mentioned here aren't limited to babies. Of course something like diapers would be; so use your common sense. But if you do have young kids, it can be applied to them as well. But if you don't have kids, do not skip this chapter because there are things in here that you really should be aware of.

Cribs and Mattresses - Natural, Organic Bedding

Did you know that a large percentage of the mattresses we sleep on every night release toxins? These toxins include a variety of plastics, polyurethane foam, arsenic, phthalates, latex/rubber, antimony, wool, biocides, phosphorus, vinyl PVC, foams, petroleum based chemicals and fire retardants. These compounds are toxic and are not stable so they continue to evaporate into the air. While we're sleeping on our mattress hour by hour, we are inhaling these toxins. The mattresses that our babies or kids sleep on are no different because they're made of the same materials; just in a smaller size. These toxins are not only harmful to our environment, but also to a child's development and immune system.

The solution is an organic crib mattress

They're made with cotton and other organic materials which are healthier for our bodies; especially our baby's body because they spend a lot of time in their cribs.

There are different manufacturers of organic crib mattresses out there. But from doing a little research I came across one that has a certified organic cotton filling and a non-toxic, natural fire protection system that's also waterproof. How about that? But one of the most important factors is that it's "greenguard" certified and does not give off gaseous, harmful chemicals which has been tested and confirmed. You can see a variety of these types of crib mattresses and crib pads at: www.livesmartinfo.com/organicmattress, which will show you Amazon's selection.

The crib's frame

Get one that has real wood with natural finishes; not the press wood because those can emit formaldehyde.

Organic Clothing

I just want to mention how amazing it is that there was a time when 100% cotton clothing was something no one dwelled on or gave a second thought to. It was just a natural thing and you could take it for granted. Not now! A lot of synthetic material for clothing has developed over the years; especially during the last century. The main ones are polyester, nylon, spandex, acrylic, rayon, acetate and triacetate. The chemicals in those materials have been linked to health problems including behavioral problems, hormone disruption and immune system damage. Are any of them in your closet or the closet of your kids?

Oh, while we're on the subject, if any of your clothing labels say no-iron, wrinkle resistant, stain proof, permanent press, static resistant or moth repellant, watch out! There are so many chemicals involved in order to label any fabric like that. One of them that totally give me the creeps is formaldehyde. It's often applied with heat so that it's trapped in the fiber permanently to prevent clothes from shrinking. Yikes!

You're probably not going to go out and throw all your existing clothes away. So here are 3 tips for you:

- If you have synthetic clothing, wash and dry them 3 times.
- **Don't dry-clean your clothes** because the chemical, perchloroethylene, is widely used by dry cleaners and is known to cause cancer in animals. Alternatively, you can frequent environmentally -friendly dry cleaners and I've noticed more of them in this 21st century. As a matter of fact, there is one in my old neighborhood that went "green" a few years ago and would've done it sooner, if it wasn't so expensive to make the change. I'm wondering if that is what's holding back other dry cleaners to do the same thing. So don't be too surprised if the cost is higher for "green" dry cleaners.
- Do you use conventional dryer sheets to reduce static cling and to soften your fabrics? If so, stop. Just stop. Start using a wonderful alternative which is a "reusable" dryer sheet. Imagine that! You can see what they look like on Amazon at www.livesmartinfo.com/reusabledryersheets. I didn't even know these were available.

The solution is natural fabric

Because natural fabrics are "natural" they not only tend to breathe better than chemically processed man-made fibers, but they keep moisture away from the body. It's so much better for your baby's skin (and yours too). You probably already know what these are. Basically it's linen, silk, cotton, cashmere, hemp and wool (although some people are allergic to wool).

Keep in mind that just because some fabrics are labeled as "natural fibers" or "cotton" doesn't mean that it wasn't treated with pesticides during its growth and sometimes it even stays put in the fiber. That's quite disturbing, isn't it? To avoid that, you and your family will need to get yourselves into organic clothing which is becoming more widely available and can be found in specialty shops, health food stores or if want, you can visit www.livesmartinfo.com/organicclothing to see what's online at Amazon in that department.

So, now that we're in the 21st century, we're searching out 100% cotton clothing, bed sheets, towels, etc. that's organic and we're paying a whole lot more money for this natural resource without pesticides. How ironic.

Eco Green Reusable Diapers

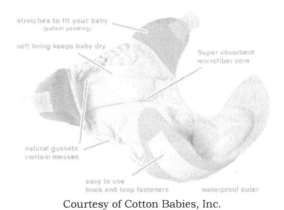

Courtesy of Cotton Babies, Inc.

When our parents were babies - depending on how old you are now - well, let me say "before" disposable diapers were available, their parents would use a piece of cotton cloth, fold it a certain way and pin it up to "make" a diaper. And if they didn't have access to a washing machine and dryer, they would hand-wash those used diapers and hang them on the clothes line to dry. Now that's more laborious and time intensive, wouldn't you say? But that's how it was and it was natural. Everyone did it and in some countries today, people are still doing it that way.

I'm just going to assume that you already know that throwing disposable diapers into the trash ends up in landfills and takes at least a couple hundred years to decompose; not to mention the chemicals contained in them that touches your baby's skin 24 hours a day. But it's convenient and we're busy, right?

Let's talk about the benefits and what's involved in using reusable cloth diapers. Many say that it's just too icky and it takes too much time and work. Who wants to bother with that? Well, we're in the 21st century and cloth diapers are more high-tech now. You don't have to "make" them anymore so it's not that challenging to make the switch. Here's a list of 8 interesting things about reusable cloth diapers:

- Instead of using safety pins to fasten them, they have built in Velcro or snaps so that's much easier to use.
- Instead of a plain ole white cloth, they come in different, naturally dyed colors and prints, friendly for your baby and the environment.
- They are both machine washable and dryable.
- If your baby has put out a load and you've got a stinky diaper, just empty it out into the toilet and flush it. Then rinse it with hot water

before laundering. That's practical, right? And it's green!

- Save yourself around $1,000 per year by using reusable diapers. Disposable ones can really add up.
- You can even get what's called "one -size pocket diapers" that you can reuse from newborn to even up to 3 years old! Just think how much money that's going to save you and how much landfill space you'll be saving too!
- There are even "cloth diaper swap groups" which can help you save money as well. You can search for those on the Internet.
- Did you know that reusable cloth diapers have resale value? Yes, you can sell them on places like eBay, www.diaperswappers.com and other marketplaces to recoup some of your initial investment. Of course it's going to depend on what condition they're in and what type or brand they are. Interesting, huh?

The specific diaper in the image above is at www.bumGenius.com. Or you can see what some different types of organic reusable baby diapers look like at www.livesmartinfo.com/organicbabydiapers which will show you what Amazon has.

So basically, making the switch from disposable to reusable diapers is just so much better on so many levels. Once you start, you'll get used to it and your baby is going to feel good about it too. He'll/She'll be thinking I'm styling in my organic, reusable underwear!

Natural Organic "Green" Toys

Babies and kids put things in their mouth all the time including their toys. It's so important that whatever they're playing with is safe. In general, people are more conscientious of that especially since the lead paint found on toys in the recent past and the danger of phthalates (pronounced THAL-ates), which are a family of industrial chemicals used as plastic softeners in different consumer products including plastic toys. The kids bite or suck on the toys and ingest this contaminate. No wonder children can get sick from playing with certain toys.

When you're considering eco-friendly toys, you want to make sure they are non-toxic and chemical-free. Some good examples of these are:

- Wood that is sustainably harvested
- Organic cotton
- Rubber wood too old to produce rubber anymore
- Recycled materials such as fabric and paper
- Bamboo which is a natural and durable material for toys

The packaging that toys come in should be taken into consideration as well. It should be recyclable and biodegradable which would be written on the box; not excessive but environmentally sensible. Look for manufacturers that are known to use innocuous organic materials when fabricating their toys because that shows they're into sustainability which is what you want. If you would like to see what some natural, organic toys looks like on Amazon, check out www.livesmartinfo.com/organictoys.

If you haven't had your baby yet and you have a baby registry, that's an excellent way to get off to a good start on getting the kind of "green" baby items that you want because YOU are the one creating the list which puts YOU in control of what comes into your home; at least for the most part anyway.

So, whether you've already had your baby or you've got one on the way, I hope the information here was practical enough for you to raise a healthy and sustainable living baby if that's the route you're considering. There's obviously a lot more areas of a baby's life that could be covered in regards to "green" options, but hopefully this is a good start!

C H A P T E R ~6~

WHAT IS "GREENWASHING"? (NO RELATION TO LAUNDRY) - ARE *YOU* BEING GREENWASHED?

After giving it some thought, I felt it was essential to include a chapter on "greenwashing" for awareness if nothing else. When making decisions on buying products that are considered to be "green", there are some things you should keep in mind so as to make a good decision both for yourself and the environment.

Listed below are 3 definitions for the meaning of "greenwashing" taken from online dictionary sources:

- "To make people believe that your company is doing more to protect the environment than it really is" - *Cambridge Dictionaries*

- "Expressions of environmentalist concerns especially as a cover for products, policies, or activities" - *Merriam-Webster's Dictionaries*

- "Disinformation disseminated by an organization so as to present an environmentally responsible public image" - *Oxford Dictionaries*

Just to give you a little background, *as quoted from Wikipedia:* **"The term "greenwashing" was coined by New York environmentalist Jay Westervelt in a 1986 essay regarding the hotel industry's practice of placing placards in each room promoting reuse of towels, ostensibly to "save the environment". Westervelt noted that, in most cases, little or no effort toward reducing energy waste was being made by these institutions - as evidenced by lack of cost reduction this practice affected."** So basically, the purpose was simply to increase their profit margin, which he deemed as disingenuous.

Now that we're in the 21st century, greenwashing has become extremely prevalent. Scores of companies have jumped on the "green" bandwagon, thus taking advantage of consumers' emotions and their wallets. How could that be?

GfK Roper Consulting, one of the world's largest consulting firms, and Yale University did a survey during the summer of 2008 which revealed a very interesting finding: "Many Americans say they are willing to pay more for "green" products. Half responded that they would "definitely" or "probably" pay 15% more for eco-friendly clothes detergent (51%) or an automobile (50%). Four in ten say they would spend 15% more on "green" computer printer paper (40%) or wood furniture (39%)." You can read the full detailed report here: http://environment.research.yale.edu/documents/downloads/a-g/GfK-Roper-Yale-Survey.pdf

Are You Overlooking Details in the Label and Ingredients?

The term "green" is meant to be BOTH ecologically-friendly and human-friendly. Almost everywhere you look these days, you'll see some sort of labeling to make you think you're buying something eco-friendly, natural or organic when in reality, you're not. Greenwashing is how companies are labeling their products to "catch your attention" and make you "feel better" about that product you're buying. But really it's a ploy to get you in most cases to pay more for the product which is obviously more profitable for them. You justify in your mind that it's "worth it" to you and that's exactly what they count on!

This isn't limited to only consumer products. It applies to foods as well whether you buy it at the store or eat out at a restaurant. Read the entire label and read all the ingredients. Don't get caught up into believing only the marketing highlights.

Look at the following examples. Have you ever seen any of these words on a product label?

- **"no trans fats"** - There are LOTS of products that didn't have any "trans fats" in the first place! But since the whole "trans fats" thing became a spectacle several years ago, the "greenwashing" just went crazy. The same products that didn't have trans fats to begin with started putting labels on their products saying "no trans fats". So when consumers see that, they start thinking oh, there are no trans fats in this product, so I can feel comfortable buying it.

- **"we use 100% vegetable oil"** - If you're eating fried foods, what kind of oil it's fried in is not more relevant than the fact that you're eating "fried" food which is not the healthiest diet. But when you see those words, you rationalize that it's not "as bad". That's what companies want you to do. They know that if the sign says "we use 100% lard", they'll probably lose customers.

- **"sugar free"** - Is the sugar being substituted with artificial sweeteners? Companies know that consumers are more health conscientious as we progress along in this 21st century. The more products they can advertise "sugar free" on, the more people will buy it. To you, it still tastes good so you're not going to worry about "why" it still tastes good. That's exactly what they want because the more you're okay with it, the more money they'll make advertising that it is sugar free.

- **"all natural"** - What really does that mean? Is it something you're willing to pay more for because it's advertised as such so that makes you feel better about it?

My Pet Peeve: "Fresh-squeezed" Orange Juice or "Fresh-squeezed" Lemonade

Now this one is personal; organic or not. I'll go back to basics here. For OJ, I go in the backyard, pick oranges off the tree and squeeze the juice out of them with a juicer (or by hand) into a glass. Now that's fresh-squeezed orange juice! For lemons, I go in the backyard, pick a few lemons off the tree, squeeze the juice out of them by hand, add water and sugar to my taste and voila! I've got fresh-squeezed lemonade. It's rare these days, in a big city, to get this anywhere. If you can find it, you'll pay an arm and a leg, and there are NO refills.

Especially for fresh-squeezed orange juice, the "greenwashing" labeling is rampant!!! From personal experience, some places use old, rotten oranges that you can't see because they do it in the back where customers can't actually see what they're doing. I cringe to wonder where the oranges are coming from and boy can I taste the difference. There's actually a bad aftertaste from old, rotting orange juice; not to mention the flavor. Not surprising.

High-end restaurants advertise "fresh-squeezed" orange juice on their menu. But when I ask if the oranges are actually on premise, I'm told they get it delivered. So they themselves really don't know what they're getting. They just know that they will charge their customers a lot more money for it.

One more thing - natural "fresh-squeezed" orange juice does not taste the same all the time. Sometimes it's tart, mild (not too flavorful), or sweet. The time of year or the type of orange determines that. So when you go to the store to buy so-called "fresh-squeezed" orange juice in the "pre-packaged" plastic containers, it is NOT fresh-squeezed orange juice because it always tastes the same no matter what time of year it is. In most cases it's pasteurized too which alters the taste as well.

BEWARE of "fresh-squeezed" orange juice labeling because unless you can see the oranges and the juicer, it's probably not what you think you're getting.

Here Are Further Examples

- **"Free of chlorofluorocarbons ("CFC")" shaving cream** marketing that makes "green" claims that are beside the point. Yes, the claim might not be fabricated. But by the same token, it's not important because CFCs have been outlawed for quite a while now. So such a claim is there simply as a marketing ploy to get over on the consumer to make him think that he's buying something that's environmentally friendly, which ultimately sells more of this shaving cream.

- **Cleaning products or laundry detergent companies** that add baking soda or enzymes to their products and advertise "clean with natural enzyme action"; but conveniently do not mention that it also has sodium laurel sulphate ("SLS" which is a skin irritant), phthalates, and other ingredients that counter the safe ones.

- **Newspapers** that claim to be green because they "offer" a section only for green advertisers but continues printing on virgin fiber paper instead of recycled.

- **Cosmetics companies** that advertise "made with vitamin E" (or Aloe Vera) and label their products as "natural", but the rest of the unnatural ingredients that it's made of remains and has not been touched.

There are so many more examples of greenwashing that I can't possibly mention them all here. But if you would like to see another 25 of them in detail with pictures, I highly recommend that you visit this link:
http://www.businesspundit.com/the-top-25-greenwashed-products-in-america/

4 Things You Can Do As a Consumer to Watch Out For "Greenwashing"

1) Get out of the comfort zone of feeling at ease just because a label contains feel-good "green" verbiage (i.e. "eco-friendly", "environmentally-friendly", "all natural", "recycled material" with a non-specified percentage, "sustainably sourced", "organic" etc.).

2) Read the full label including the FINE print on the back to make sure you do not see anything that makes you skeptical. In most cases, the fewer substances you have to question the more likely the product is up to par.

3) Get comfortable asking the seller or supplier of a product what an ingredient is that you're not sure about. Nowadays, most of these companies have a website or a phone number that you can call that's printed on the label. If you're in a food/restaurant environment, ask the cook or manager what they're putting in the food if you're not sure. I want to specifically mention that if you see the word "organic" instead of "certified organic", ask the manufacturer what that means.

4) Look for some type of product certification which is better than no certification at all. This shows that the manufacturer was willing to go through a formal certification process. Of course that's not fool-proof but it is something to keep in mind.

Here are a couple product certification sources: (a) Scientific Certification Systems ("SCS") - For various levels of environmental performance, they certify fish, food, flowers, electricity, wood products and manufactured goods. Their "Indoor Advantage" certification guarantees that products used indoors have minimal or no volatile organic compounds ("VOC"); check out www.scscertified.com. **(b)** Green Guard - They certify indoor products and low-emission building materials; check out www.greenguard.org.

In conclusion, don't obsess over finding out if a label or advertisement is greenwashing you. Just keep the things mentioned above in mind along with a healthy curiosity.

With more "greenwashing" consumer awareness, governmental agencies will increasingly crack down on it. But there are companies quite genuine in their "green" endeavors. They're seeing the positive trickledown effect it has on both consumers and the environment; not to mention other companies that don't want to look bad, so they'll follow suit to spare themselves from the negative spotlight if nothing else.

C H A P T E R ~7~

REUSABLE GROCERY BAGS - AN ECO-FRIENDLY ALTERNATIVE

Courtesy of Project GreenBag

By now, you've probably seen reusable bags around at grocery stores. And many other stores (drugstores, liquor stores, convenience stores, etc.) are using them too and even their name is printed on them.

It was inevitable that reusable bags would eventually come into play during this 21st century due to landfills infested with disposable plastic bags, which of course are not environmentally friendly. Sometimes you can see them floating and blowing around the streets and the highways; totally irresponsible! Plastic bags also end up in the ocean and harm marine and wildlife because they mistake it for food and unintentionally eat it which can kill them. We're at a point now where we need to change our shopping bag habits.

If you travel to an underprivileged country, outside of the tourist areas, they don't provide free plastic bags abundantly like they do in the western world. You'll carry your shopping goods in your hands if you don't BYOB - bring your own bag! When you look around, you'll see the natives carrying their own shopping bags to put their goods in. That's what I call non-choice natural conservation; no wasting!

My Little Grocery Bag Story

For years - I would say no less than a decade ago - I would recycle my "paper in plastic" (double) grocery bags. For me, it wasn't a matter of "going green". It was the fact that I hated seeing the bags stack up. I was running out of space in the cupboard where I kept them and it just bugged me that these bags kept accumulating.

To do something about it, I started keeping them in the trunk of my car. I would bring my groceries into the kitchen, sometimes 9 double bags at a time, and then after unpacking them I would neatly fold them up and put them in the trunk of my car for my next grocery store visit.

I shopped at the same stores every week and I did not see other customers doing the same thing (reusing their grocery bags). Sometimes the cashiers would say that more customers should be doing this. After a while, grocery stores started giving 3 to 5 cents for every bag that was being reused. So I was getting paid for reusing bags that I was going to reuse anyway until they literally tore apart! More people caught on to that so grocery stores began offering points instead and no more cash (although I think a few still might). These days, monetary incentives are not as readily offered; instead "encouragement" to reuse your bags because it helps out the environment is.

Not All Reusable Grocery Bags Are the Same

I'm going to focus on reusable bags relating to grocery shopping because it's the most common and has the most impact.

Reusable bags come in different materials. People have their individual preferences as to which one is best for them. Despite the material you choose for your reusable bag, the bigger picture is that you are potentially keeping loads of plastic bags from polluting the environment. And for paper shopping bags, beyond its biodegradability, you're saving trees. So let's explore some makes of reusable grocery bags.

Reusable organic cotton canvas bags - These are the most eco-friendly. Their cotton is high-quality, its capacity is that of a paper bag and they are sturdy. Some of them have built-in compartments for holding bottles, milk containers or taller items which makes it convenient. And the handles are long enough to put over your shoulders which can free up your hands to carry additional bags. These do cost more than the others. But they're washable, long lasting and come in solid earthy colors.

Reusable nylon bags - These are the easiest to remember to carry with you especially for spontaneous or last-minute grocery store trips. That's because they're not as sturdy which means you can ball them up and stick them anywhere; in your purse or even in a jacket pocket (although I would attempt to fold it). They're stretchy and durable and hard to tell that they were balled up once you've filled them with groceries. You can wash them in cold water and let them air dry. Some even come with a shoulder pad so that you can carry it over your shoulder if you prefer.

Reusable mesh bags for produce - Yes! There are even reuse smaller bags for your fruits and vegetables. These mesh bags are easy to see through (just as you can a produce plastic bag), they have a drawstring, are stretchable, there's air circulation, and are the same size as a usual plastic produce bag. You can conveniently wash the produce right in the bag because of the mesh holes. Although they hardly weigh anything, just ask the checker to subtract its weight. These come in both cotton and polyester. You can keep your produce stored in it in the refrigerator, on the counter, or in the pantry. But I would use the cotton ones for storage. You can see what's out there on Amazon in terms of reusable grocery and produce bags at www.livesmartinfo.com/reusablegrocerybags.

More and more stores are selling reusable bags with their own logo or name printed on them. I've seen some and they're pretty cheap looking. However, if you buy one from a health food store, they're usually pretty good. Although some people don't mind, depending on where they shop, another store's pre-printed logo or name on the reusable bag might not be tasteful, so to speak. But again, the most important thing is that you are reusing it.

4 Practical Tips for Reusable Grocery Bags

1. Wash your reusable grocery bags to keep bacteria from building up from raw meat, fish or produce.

2. If you want to go to the extent, it might be helpful to label them so that you're using the same bag for like items (cleaning supplies, dairy products, meat, etc.).

3. REMEMBERING TO BRING THEM! We've been so conditioned over the years to walk into a store empty handed and just take for granted that we'll be provided a bag when we buy something. To get into a "green" habit, here's what to do:

(a) If you have a car, keep these bags in it (glove compartment, trunk, side pocket, etc.). Although I kept reusable bags in the trunk of my car, sometimes I would forget to bring them into the market with me. But when I realized it, I would let out a growl, and then go out to my car and get them from the trunk. This was part of my re-conditioning.

(b) If you have the ones that you can ball up and you carry a purse, stuff a couple of them in there.

(c) If there's a jacket that you often wear, put it in one of the pockets so that you'll have it handy.

4. FOR MEN! I've noticed that reusable bags in general are more geared toward females. You hear about patterns, colors of the bag, etc. It's usually females concerned with that. I want you guys to know that men can use reusable grocery bags too. It's not a female thing. It's an environmental thing. When I see a man using a reusable bag, he gets a thumbs-up. And when I see a man using a reusable "produce" bag, it's like WOW! I'd like to see more men putting this in action. It sets a good, positive example that men should be doing this too. Just get a neutral tan color and avoid bright colors if that holds you back or makes you uncomfortable. But please don't let that stop you from getting into this habit. And tell your male friends to get on board with this too!

It's just a matter of getting into the routine and changing your mindset. Once you start, it gets easier. It's amazing how other people will see you with a reusable grocery bag and feel guilty. Over the years I've had numerous individuals commend me and say that's what they should be doing too. But more and more people are doing it now.

Don't limit yourself to just grocery stores. Bring your reusable bags to "every" store. Get in the habit and it'll rub off on other people (even if it's only because they feel guilty)!

How About Condensing or Using No Bag At All for Small Stuff?

Condensing - When you go grocery shopping, have you noticed that there's very little or no attempt by the bagger to get everything into one bag? Instead, they put three or four items in the "plastic" bag and then grab another "plastic" bag to add additional items to when the first bag could've easily held them. It's wasteful, thoughtless and bad for the landfills.

To help curb this occurrence, simply let the cashier know that you would like everything in "one" bag if possible. If it turns out to be unreasonably heavy, it's okay to use an additional bag to distribute the weight more evenly. The point is that you are being responsible. The cashier or bagger has to then put in a little thought and eco-friendly effort into how things are being packed. For them, taking the easy route is easier; but it contributes to the problem.

No bag at all - When you have additional stops to make after your first one and you already have a bag in your car that's not 100% full, don't let that extra space in the bag go to waste. If there are 1, 2 or maybe even 3 additional small items that you need to buy at your next stop, tell the cashier "No bag please!" Then carry those items in your hand and put them in the bag that's not full. You'll not only use up that extra space in the existing bag, but you'll be sparing the landfills from unnecessary extra "plastic" bags floating around out there.

Collectively, just doing these two simple things alone, especially if you're not using a reusable bag, can really make a difference if more people would just do it and encourage others to do the same. As mentioned earlier, once you get into the habit, it becomes second nature.

C H A P T E R ~8~

ORGANIC COSMETICS - A RISING PREFERENCE

Courtesy of Roberrific

The average American woman uses all kinds of different cosmetics. You might be one of them. Did you know that you'll end up absorbing 4 pounds of chemicals from those products over a lifetime? The public health laws aren't written as well as they should be which allows cosmetic companies to use almost any kind of chemicals they want, thus taking advantage of loopholes. This is not limited to adults. Children and babies are affected by it with shampoos and other products used on them because petrochemicals absorbs into their system.

Why Switch To Green Cosmetics?

Switch to Green Cosmetics for the health of yourself, your family, and the environment. Let's see what's involved.

Petrochemicals are chemicals derived from petroleum (crude oil) and natural gas. A large variety of products that most people interact with daily are made using it which includes detergents, soaps, flooring, solvents, epoxies, plastics (used in the construction of a steering wheel), synthetic fibers (used in fleece jackets), fertilizers, pesticides, rubber, pharmaceuticals, rubber, and other materials.

Only about 10% of our cosmetics are even looked at by the Cosmetic Ingredient Review or the FDA or anyone else. But just in case you aren't sure that there's dangerous stuff in there, let's look more closely to what kinds of dangers lurk in the ingredients.

For example, placental extracts from animals are an important ingredient in our skin and hair products. When a product advertises glowing skin and hair, this is what they use to deliver on that promise. The only problem is that these extracts come with a bunch of hormones. After you put on something that is made of placental extracts, if you were to touch your baby, your baby gets a dose of it too. And it can play havoc with his/her health.

Remember the huge deal made over lead in paint used on Thomas The Tank Engine toys imported from China? Well mercury happens to be even more poisonous. It can cause brain damage – especially in children. They don't actually list mercury as such in any cosmetic product. They instead list it by the name of the mercury compound they use which is termed "thimerosal". You'd be looking pretty hard to find a mainstream cosmetic product that didn't have this. Even contact lens solutions have this. (Gee whiz, no wonder back in the day when I used to wear contact lenses I used to have a hard time finding a solution that I wasn't allergic to.)

Perfume and fragrance is used in practically every product. The only problem is that fragrances contain toxins. They are about the worst allergy producing things ever. This is one of the reasons why we keep hearing about autoimmune diseases so much these days.

Plastic Cosmetic Packaging

You probably don't think much about the container your cosmetics is packaged in; but packaging is a major factor. The entire packaging lifecycle must have minimal environmental impact in order to be considered as "sustainable". Think about it; let's use a tube of lipstick for example which is packaged in a plastic container. Once you've twisted the bottom of it upwards as far as it will go and used the exposed portion, if you aren't willing to start using a lip brush to dig down into the part that won't twist up any further, you're not going to get any more lipstick out of that plastic tube. But the question is: Are you willing to take the time to do that to prolong throwing it into the trash bin? This means you'll have to carry *both* your tube of lipstick along with a lip brush. No it's not as convenient; but it's less wasteful and you'd be getting your money's worth instead of throwing it away half-used thus contributing that plastic container to a landfill sooner than you otherwise would have.

I used that example because back in the 80s, I used to be appalled at how much of my lipstick I couldn't get to because it was at or just under the plastic container's edge. For me, it wasn't a green cosmetics thing. I just couldn't stand the thought of throwing away all the lipstick that was still in there. So even since back then I carried in my purse a lip brush and used it to dig out the lipstick and I mean every drop! It really did last longer too before having to buy another one (of my favorite color).

There is a biodegradable plastic or "bioplastic" made of polyhydroxyalkanoates ("PHAs") which are naturally occurring bacterial products that would be ideal for cosmetic packaging and do not require the consumption of fossil fuels as feedstock. But there is a production process involved that right now isn't as economically competitive with petroleum-based plastics. However, to make PHA products more commercially available, further research and advances are being made toward bringing this about.

Food-based Personal Care Products on the Rise

Many cosmetic packaging manufacturers have resorted to fair trade which means that more and more food based ingredients will be used to provide functionality in personal care products. Food-based ingredients are becoming a popular choice for companies transitioning to organic and natural based cosmetic products and right now there are no signs of slowing down. Especially for companies that are looking to profit from new and innovative strategies, these trends serve as an important building block.

These manufacturers have realized that sustainability is not an eco-band aid, so to speak. They have started forcing businesses to become active throughout the production cycle. Cosmetic companies are using everything from eco-friendly packaging to innovative product formulations to garner a greater environmentally friendly image for their products.

Some of the food ingredients in personal care products include soy (both isoflavones & protein), pomegranate curcumin, olive oil and green tea; among others. I thought this website was really interesting for "homemade" cosmetic recipes if you're really interested in going 100% natural: http://safecosmetics.org/article.php?id=233.

If you haven't already, read the Greenwashing chapter in this book. It complements awareness about organic cosmetics fraud which is another thing to keep in mind as you read advertisements and ingredients contained in your personal care products. There is more about that here: http://www.organicconsumers.org/bodycare/index.cfm

Where Can I Find Green or Eco-Cosmetics Right Now?

Eventually, it will be easier to find fully green, eco-friendly cosmetics at your neighborhood drug store. But for now, you can find some of them online. Listed below are some of the more common cosmetic items currently available at Amazon:

- **Lipstick** - www.livesmartinfo.com/organiclipstick
- **Mascara** - www.livesmartinfo.com/organicmascara
- **Eye Shadow** - www.livesmartinfo.com/organiceyeshadow
- **Blush** - www.livesmartinfo.com/organicblush

- **Eye Liner** -
  www.livesmartinfo.com/organiceyeliner
- **Facial Cream** -
  www.livesmartinfo.com/organicfacialcream
- **Liquid Foundation** -
  www.livesmartinfo.com/organicliquidfoundation
- **Nail Polish** -
  www.livesmartinfo.com/organicnailpolish

The packaging for these products is not quite green yet; but the ingredients are all natural. At least you won't find petroleum byproducts in them. The next best cosmetics packaging available right now is made from glass. But as mentioned earlier, it's a work in progress.

The subject of "green" packaging has become a hot topic due to consumer demand and government insistence. More green cosmetic solutions are on the horizon and we know that it's healthier for us and our families as well as the environment.

RESOURCES:

Search these words on the Internet: "white paper cosmetic sustainability pdf "
- http://www.fda.gov/Cosmetics/default.htm
- http://www.cosmeticsinfo.org/safety.php

CHAPTER ~9~

SOLAR POWER FOR SUSTAINABLE LIVING - WHAT TO CONSIDER *BEFORE* GOING THE DO IT YOURSELF SOLAR ROUTE

Courtesy of joncallas

There has been a spike in interest over renewable energy worldwide in the form of solar energy, among others; especially during this 21st century. Renewable energy in its rawest form is the sun, oceans, wind, heat deep within the earth, lakes, plant growth and rivers. By converting these natural endless resources into the form of electricity, heat for our homes, heat for water and transportation fuels, modern technology continues to demonstrate the potential for replacement of finite resources currently being used.

This is a major topic of discussion for economists, governments and environmentalists. There are many reasons for this but two of the main ones are: (1) Utility costs (electricity, heating, water & gas) continue to increase making sustainable energy an attractive alternative to fossil fuels and other non-renewable sources and (2) Harnessing clean renewable energy or "green" energy is simply better for the environment and cuts down on greenhouse gases and carbon footprints.

New technologies in the field of renewable energy continue to be developed and many want to take full advantage of this. We will focus on solar power because there is such a great interest in this particular form or energy right now. There are some new and interesting options that you may not be aware of as yet, but might want to explore further.

What Exactly Is Solar Power and How Does it Work?

Solar power is the conversion of sunlight or solar energy into electricity. A popular "active" solar technique used to do this is the direct use of photovoltaic ("PV") panels as a means of harnessing that energy. Solar thermal collectors, pumps and fans for the conversion of sunlight into useful outputs can also be used. But we will focus mostly on the former.

Considering that **photovoltaic (PV) power generation** is a technique greatly involved for taking advantage of this energy, having a closer look at it will broaden your understanding of how the process works. Photovoltaic (PV) power generation uses solar panels which are made of many solar cells that contain photovoltaic material such as crystalline silicon (aka C-Si or solar grade silicon). A PV "system" uses at *least* one solar panel for conversion of sunlight into electricity, which involves various components such as mountings, photovoltaic modules (solar panels), means of modifying or regulating the electrical output, and mechanical & electric connections.

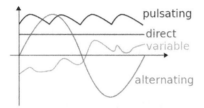

A single PV module or **solar panel** rarely produces enough power to meet the requirements of a home (or business), so the panels are linked together to form what's called a solar array (or PV array). These are attached together in series to get the voltage you want. Each string is connected in parallel which allows the system to produce more electric current. In most cases, there's an electricity grid that the electricity is fed into using a power inverter to convert the direct current (DC) power that it produced by the panels, which isn't usable, into alternating current (AC) which can power lights, motors, and other items that we can use. There are power inverters that include an LED display which keeps track and monitors the system's performance. There are many kinds of inverters and you can see Amazon's selection of them at www.livesmartinfo.com/inverters.

In standalone systems, energy or electricity that is not immediately needed is stored in batteries and can be used to recharge or power portable devices. It can also be fed into a large electricity grid that's powered by central generation plants; even combined with domestic electricity generators to feed into a smaller sized grid.

A photovoltaic cell (or **solar cell**) is an electrical device that converts the energy of light directly into electricity via the photovoltaic effect (which is the creation of electric current or voltage in a material when exposed to light). Solar cells are often encapsulated (via protective waterproof enclosure) as a module or solar panel. Or there could be a sheet of glass on the sun-up front side so that light can pass while still protecting the semiconductor wafer (aka "slice") from getting scratched by wind-driven debris or rained upon, etc.

How to Figure Out If a Photovoltaic (PV) Solar Energy System Is Conducive For You - Get an Answer for 6 Questions!

It's not going to be cost effective or a wise investment to have PV panels installed as a means of lowering your utility bills (or eventually getting rid of them altogether) if enough solar power isn't being generated per month to cover your household utility costs. This means you'll need to calculate beforehand some information regarding costs, output, etc.

1) What is your average monthly energy consumption? Gather your last 12 month's utility bills to figure out your household's average kilowatt hours ("kWh") per month. This is how much electricity was actually used on the average per month. Once you know this information, you'll be able to determine the minimum amount of solar power generation needed in order to meet your household's requirements.

2) What is your geographic location? In the United States, there are photovoltaic solar radiation resource maps (see Resource #1) that provide monthly average (and annual) daily totals from PV panels that are oriented due south. The map can give you an idea potentially of the solar radiation power to be expected from the sun. In reference to "kWh/m²/day" on the map, m = PV cell (or absorber area) put into square meters. The size of each panel, strong sunlight, and length of daily sunray exposure all have a bearing on how much electricity is produced. If you live outside the U.S., try searching online for this type of map in your country or region.

3) What makes up the cost of a Photovoltaic (PV) System? There are many factors that go into determining that cost once you have the answers to the first two questions above. A couple of things that should be considered is the cost of the system size depending on how many kilowatt hours you need for your home, and of course labor or installation cost (which in some cases could be double the cost of the system). Just to give you an idea, here's an example from somewhere in the US: During the summer of 2011, company ABC offered a medium sized system that could generate 480 kWh per month for around $9,000 with no incentives. But when incentives were involved, the system itself cost around $6,000, without installation. The cost will vary because every situation is customized and tailored.

Something you can do is to call "several" local *experienced* solar panel installation contractors for an estimate and compare what each of them would charge you. Have them come to your home or building and do an on-site assessment. You won't be obligated and don't let them talk you into doing anything; just get as much information out of them as you can. This is important because contractors and their grandmothers were jumping on the solar installation bandwagon and some of them weren't properly licensed to do the work. So make sure they have a contractor's license, general liability, and worker's compensation because if something happens while they're on that roof you do not want to be responsible.

Another practical thing that you can do is drive around your neighborhood and if you see a house that has solar panels on its roof top (you can't miss it), knock on the door to ask your neighbor some questions or leave a little note letting them know that you live close by in the neighborhood and you're considering getting solar panels and wanted to know how it was working out for them. Ask if they did it themselves or used a company. If so, which company? If it's comfortable, ask how much it cost them to do it themselves or to have it done. Are they pleased with how it's serving them? Write down your address and phone number so that they can get in touch with you. Tell them your concerns or apprehensions about getting a PV system. You would be surprised at how willing folks are to talk about something in common.

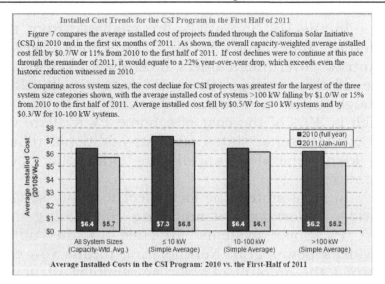

Average Installed Costs in the CSI Program: 2010 vs. the First-Half of 2011

4) What about guarantees and post-installation? Although solar panels can last around 20 years or more, have no moving parts, can withstand inclement weather conditions (if properly installed), and does not require much maintenance aside from an inspection now and then to remove leaves, bird droppings, dirt, etc., it is still not a bad idea to use a company that has some sort of ongoing quality assurance, guarantee or post-installation support.

5) What incentives are offered for users of PV solar systems? There are government incentives including tax credits, rebates or subsidies available to help offset the cost of installed PV solar systems for both residential and commercial buildings. These are in place because they realize that at this time, it is a substantial investment. However, as PV system prices steadily decline, it's inevitable that subsidies will not be offered; taking into consideration grid parity (which is when the cost of solar competes favorably with gird prices without incentives) eventually coming into play.

In the US, incentives are available from the Federal, State and Local jurisdictions. (Other country's government offers incentives too.) At the time of this writing, there is currently in place through 2016 a Federal Investment Tax Credit which is 30% of the cost of a home PV system. On top of that, some states offer an additional rebate per kWh generated, and larger cities offer local incentives.

In most states, the local electric utility service providers allow for **net-metering** considering that most PV solar systems are tied to the utility provider's power grid. Net-metering means you can subtract the amount of solar power kilowatt hours that you produce during the daylight hours from your overall electrical usage each billing period and only pay the difference or a reduced amount to the utility company. Any excess energy that you produce for the month feeds into the utility company's grid which means it's possible to not have to pay anything at all and maybe even get paid by the utility company for the excess. However, not every state allows it to be unlimited as some do have a limit on how much they'll allow to be subtracted. You may visit http://en.wikipedia.org/wiki/Net_metering to see a list of which states allow for how much net-metering. Don't forget to ask your electric utility company for a special backward-spinning meter. The more backwards it spins the more solar energy you're gaining!

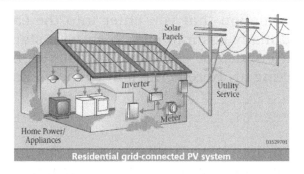

Residential grid-connected PV system

If you have more of an interest in an off-grid PV solar system, which means not being connected to a utility company at all, which is doable, the installation process has different necessities considering electric power requirements need to be met during cloudy conditions and at night. This includes a bank of batteries, which are extremely expensive and only lasts for about 6 years, a charge controller, and in most cases, an inverter.

6) Are there any free resources to help me estimate what this PV system will cost me? Yes! There's an excellent website that's a free public service of the solar and wind communities and a recommended resource by the National Renewable Energy Laboratory (NREL) and the U.S. Department of Energy (DOE).

- Their free **Solar and Wind Estimator** can be used for both the US and CANADA. It estimates both the size and cost to install an energy system for a home or building. The energy systems also include space heating & cooling, solar water heating, wind turbines, and pool or spa heating. It also provides a financial analysis based upon expected energy bill savings and the net system cost after applying incentives and tax credits. It is only an estimate based upon the limited information that you enter into the calculator and many assumptions. It's just a start to give you an idea or estimate of what you might be looking at. Here is the link to the estimator: http://www.solar-estimate.org/index.php?page=solar-calculator

- Its proprietary databases carry the industry's largest and most up-to-date **incentives and rebates for solar and wind energy** for the US. This includes any new federal, state, local and utility incentives as well as rebates and financing options that can help you pay for solar and wind power systems. Here is the link: http://www.solar-estimate.org/index.php?page=taxcredit

- Another helpful resource is the Database of State Incentives for Renewables & Efficiency - http://www.dsireusa.org/ - which is a **comprehensive source of information on state, local, utility, federal incentives** and policies that promote renewable energy & energy efficiency. I highly recommend taking a look at it to find out what your state can offer you.

- This resource mentioned here is so invaluable because you can **prescreen local solar and wind contractors**, as well as energy professionals by name or enter a zip code to find one near you in both the US and CANADA. You'll be able to see their experience and track record and verify if they are licensed, bonded and not financially on their way out, so to speak. You can also view their professional and customer references. Here is the link:

http://www.solar-estimate.org/index.php?page=solar-installer

Overall, all the information and calculations will give you a rough estimate as to how long it could take you to pay off a PV system as it will vary in the number of years.

DIY (Do It Yourself) PV Solar System Installation - What You Ought To Know!

Roof Area Needed in Square Feet (shown in Bold Type)							
PV Module Efficiency (%)	PV Capacity Rating (Watts)						
	100	250	500	1,000	2,000	4,000	10,000
4	30	75	150	300	600	1,200	3,000
8	15	38	75	150	300	600	1,500
12	10	25	50	100	200	400	1,000
16	8	20	40	80	160	320	800

For example, to generate 2,000 watts from a 12%-efficient system, you need 200 square feet of roof area.

Why is there tremendous interest in DIY PV solar system installation during this 21st Century? That's a no-brainer. It's TOO EXPENSIVE for most people to get it professionally done by a contractor - even with all the incentives that's being offered. Yes, the cost has been coming down gradually. But it's still too cost prohibitive to have a professional come out and take care of it. That's why these DIY Solar Kits are really popular, and in demand. It's going to be an expense either way you slice it. So let's get into what's really involved here.

In the US, almost all installed photovoltaic solar systems are tied into the local utility company's grid. If that's what you have in mind as well, it's a good idea before getting started to contact your utility company to get permission and specifications for tying your system into their grid (net metering) for offsetting your utility costs. And in regards to the current (as of this writing) 30% Federal Investment Tax Credit program, confirm that your do-it-yourself solar kit meets the program's guidelines because you don't want to have done all the work just to find out afterward that you don't qualify for that rebate!

What does a DIY solar power kit cost? The price for solar panel kits can range anywhere from $100 to $10,000 depending on the number of solar panels you'll need, the amount of wattage that needs to be generated, where you buy it from, length of warranty for specific items, etc. The more high-end and "complete" with goodies that come in the kit, the more it's going to cost you.

Each kit will have detailed 'specifications' (or specs) so that you know exactly what you're getting. These specs need to match up with what your needs are. They will not come with every single thing. You are going to have to buy some things separately, so be prepared for that. For instance, maybe a more inexpensive kit doesn't include a power inverter and/or some other necessary components; but that's the way they keep the price affordable. You will still need to buy a power inverter. You know how it is - you get what you pay for.

What comes inside a DIY solar power kit? A DIY solar power kit should include everything you need (in correspondence with how much you spend on it). NOTE: This is not an exhaustive list; but it is the basic main components.

- **PV Solar Panel** - the largest piece in the kit; should generate a minimum of 80 watts and allow for "add-on" future panels to generate additional electricity if you find later on that you're not getting enough with what you have already installed

- **Solar Panel Stand** - lets you adjust the angle to allow for the maximum amount of sun exposure; ideally 70 degrees on your roof top
- **Rechargeable Battery** - should be 85 Ah
- **Charger Controller** - lets the current trickle through without spikes that can blow out appliances (very important)
- **Waterproof Box** for battery and controller - this allows for protection from the elements while being stored outside
- **Power Inverter (or latest technology Micro-Inverter)** - (from D/C to A/C) kept inside and should be at least 300 watts for any decent use. Plug a power strip into its outlet and then you can plug in your small appliances for use. It can also be hooked up to heat water.
- **Watt Meter** - see how much power is being used
- **Mounting Hardware** - includes rail, ground lugs, 4" standoffs, and clamps (for asphalt shingle roofs)
- **Wiring**
- **Solar Battery Charger**
- **Battery cables**
- **Breaker**
- **Nuts, Bolts & Screws**
- **Videos, Illustrations and Complete Instructions**

Additional materials that you can get from the hardware store if it's not included in the kit are:

- Plexiglas
- Silicon Rubber Caulking
- Aluminum Sheet
- Epoxy
- Electric Tape
- Fiberboard
- Aluminum Bar Stock

Tools you will most likely need to use:

- Hand Drill
- Exacto Knife
- Hacksaw
- Caulking gun
- Multimeter
- Soldering Iron
- Ruler
- Pencil

What is the best DIY Solar Panel Instruction Guide? Although your DIY solar panel kit is supposed to come with instructions on how to set it up, the instructions might be missing or you might find the instructions difficult to follow. Alternatively, you can buy one and immediately download it. There are many to choose from; but for your convenience, here are 3 popular ones: *Power 4 Home, Green DIY Energy, and Earth 4 Energy*

Apparently, *Green DIY Energy* seems to be the favorite because although it cost $50, it also comes with a money-back guarantee and their tutorial videos and instructions are easy to understand and follow. It even covers how to assemble components even if you have no electricity experience.

Where Can I Get FREE Help and Advice For DIY Solar Panel Installation?

Local Services - Contact your utility company. Check around to see if your community offers materials and workshops for DIY homemade solar cells. Maybe call up a solar panel installation company and ask them how to use a specific related item.

Online Forums - You can learn so much from visiting online forums related to solar panels. You would be amazed at how much real, hands-on information you'll find. The members on the forum are passionate about the subject matter. They talk about what they've experienced when it comes to installing solar panels, give recommendations, tips, things not to do, etc. Almost always there's an expert member that's glad to reply to your questions. Other members that might know the answer will reply as well. Think of it as a "solar panel community" that you can actively get involved with as you make progress. The one that I find to be very informative and instructional is at www.solarpaneltalk.com/.

YouTube - Search YouTube for videos on how to build a PV solar panel system. There are thousands of them that you can watch! Weed out the ones that might not pinpoint exactly what you need to know by typing into the search box specifically what you want to know or do. For instance, if you're not sure how to apply epoxy to encapsulate a solar cell, type these specific words into the YouTube search box like this: "how to apply epoxy to encapsulate a solar cell". Include the quotation marks too! It's a lot of words, but it's more specific and will help narrow down the video search results so that you can spend your time efficiently.

What Else Should I Keep In Mind Regarding DIY Solar Panel Systems?

- There's a resource (mentioned earlier) on how to calculate kWh as well as what to do to find out what you need to know before spending money on anything really.
- Make sure you've done your research beforehand so that you know exactly what size kit to buy and that you can obtain ALL the materials and tools necessary before starting because you'll be held up if you're missing parts and things.
- Read in advance to make sure you understand everything from an instruction guide. If you can't get past what you don't understand at the time you're reading the instructions, you're going to come across the same thing once you actually start doing the work.
- Hold on to all your receipts for each and every thing you buy related to your project as you might end up needing them later on.

When setting up a DIY Solar Panel System, you will be working with many technical and safety issues. If you have enough experience with home improvement projects and are comfortable working on a rooftop, you should be able get this done just fine. However, have a licensed electrician assist you with the electrical part of the installation and final configuration.

So, whether you're an expert do-it-yourselfer or just starting out, bringing a DIY solar panel system to fruition for your home is certainly doable and might even be fun. If you can afford to go the professional installation route, that's fine too. The end result is the same which is to employ clean, renewable energy as a means of generating electricity and keeping utility cost to a minimum.

What Is Residential Solar Leasing About?

The new thing that's coming on the horizon is residential solar leasing which can also be referred to as solar rental programs, solar financing, or solar power purchase agreements. You are able to lease solar panels for your home instead of spending the upfront money to buy them. For those who want to generate clean energy for their home but can't afford to buy a photovoltaic solar system even with incentives, leasing is the new solution.

It works the same as with any leasing program. You obviously will not own the PV solar system; the leasing company will. That also means the leasing company gets to reap the solar incentives including the 30% tax credit, rebates, etc. But you'll get free installation and zero upfront cost. Or you'll have the option to put a down-payment of $1,000 (or whatever amount) to have a lower leasing cost because you'll still be getting your monthly utility bill as well; but you'll be saving about 5% to 25%, which varies of course. The difference is that with a solar lease, you'll be locked into a contract for 10, 15 or 20 years. This means that when your electricity bill increases (historically around 6%), your solar lease bill will remain the same or only increase +/-2%. It's getting a little challenging to find leasing companies that will lock in a fixed rate for the term of the lease.

They do need to see if you'll qualify for a lease which includes living in a state where solar energy is more conducive, having a south facing roof that has a large space without obstructions and a good roof angle.

As far as maintenance, aside from occasionally washing the panels and possibly replacing the inverter, there's nothing else to it. They will also have a monitoring system installed to indicate when or if the system has been compromised in any way so that they can immediately come out and remedy it.

Once your lease is up, you can renew the agreement, cancel or even buy the system. If you cancel, the equipment will be removed by the leasing company at no cost to you. But what if you need to sell your home or move before your lease expires? Well, that's something to consider. Hopefully the buyer (or renter) will be favorable to leasing solar panels.

If leasing a solar system interests you, here is a partial list of companies nationwide in alphabetical order that you can look up on the Internet for more information and their contact form:

- Centrosolar
- Citizenre
- Connecticut Solar Lease
- Solar City
- Solar Universe
- Sun Edison
- Sungevity
- SunRun
- The Sunpower Lease

There are additional companies that you can locate by contacting either a solar contractor or your local utility provider. Although in today's dollars, 20 years of lease payments will add up to more than it would cost to just buy a PV solar system. But you won't have the massive upfront cost to deal with and you don't have to do-it-yourself either. There are pros and cons to everything, isn't there?

How Are Solar Roof Shingles (aka Solar Tiles) Different from Solar Panels?

Courtesy of Mira66

Photovoltaic roof shingles are aesthetically pleasing in comparison to large, bulky solar panels (like the picture on the left) because they are sleek-looking (seamless style), come in dark blue or black, and are just as energy efficient. Do you consider solar panels to be eye sores? When you see solar panels on a house's rooftop, do you find that you stare at them? It's like a combination of "awe and do they have to look so conspicuous"? Well, there's an alternative for that which is called solar roof shingles (or tiles) which is textured to compliment the granular surface of conventional asphalt shingles. They accomplish the same purpose as solar panels, which is to convert the sun's radiation into clean energy to power your house.

Courtesy of Jhritz

They can last longer than regular roofing tiles because they lie flat against the surface (like the picture on the left (on the *right* side.) They're actually layered onto the roof deck, nailed in place, and wired together through pre-drilled holes. Their backing is typically stainless steel sheet metal and a minimum of 5 inches of the durable photovoltaic thin film-covered surface is exposed. Solar shingles are considered a *type* of building-integrated PV, which can extend the life of your roof. Think of it as solar-generating building material, or specialized solar shingles that can endure high winds and also serve as a protection from the elements.

Because of their low profile, heavy brackets or roof penetration is not required. Their size can be rectangular about 12 inches wide by 86.5 inches long, or can be square too. Across each cell, bypass diodes are connected which enables the modules to produce power even if shaded partially. During installation, each and every module must be perfectly connected together because if one piece of wire connection is missing, the solar system will not work. The installers need to really know what they're doing.

Interestingly, the sun's heat fuses all the shingles together which forms a barrier that's water-tight. Also, by its nature, solar tiles stay cooler allowing for high efficiency at all times.

Just a side note for solar panels in general - if you're in an area where they could be covered with snow, just use a garden hose to spray the modules with water and then use a rubber squeegee blade that you can stick on the end of a broom stick to easily wipe them off.

The downsides:

- Pricing is more expensive for a solar shingles/tiles system than for a regular solar panel system.
- It's more labor intensive because of its intricacy.
- If you have a larger array, expect to pay more for installation.
- Make sure you have a warranty because if for some reason it stops working, both a solar integrator and a metal roofer will have to scope out the problem and they each could charge up to $100 per hour. If you have a large array it'll take even longer to find the source of the problem.

Other than that, they really are more attractive than the usual solar panels and will surely increase your property value. Taking advantage of available incentives should help!

How Do Solar Pool Covers Work?

Solar pool covers is another aspect of how solar energy can be used to keep swimming pools heated. The cost of heating a swimming pool can make your utility bill go up during off-peak summer months. But fortunately there's a "solar" way to take care of that by using a solar pool cover, which is less expensive than traditional pool covers. There are several different types to choose from depending on what's most convenient for you and what your preference is.

1) Regular Solar Blanket - Think of a regular solar blanket as like a big bubble wrap protected by strong vinyl on each side that serves as an insulating layer over the surface of your pool trapping the warmth of the sunshine into your pool. Let's say you already have a pool heater that you turned on for a while, this solar blanket will help retain the heat in the water from escaping into the atmosphere which means you won't need to run the heater as long and that'll save you money; especially during winter.

You don't need to anchor or tie it down because it's designed to float on the surface of the pool and if you have the proper size for your pool, it can be completely covered. It usually comes with a cover reel that makes it easy to roll the cover off of the pool, or you can just pull it off. Then fold it and store it if you'd like.

They come in a reflective blue color or clear. The clear ones really maximize the sun's heat and can raise water temperature even by as much as 15 degrees. But they do cost a little more comparatively speaking. You can see what they look like on Amazon at www.livesmartinfo.com/solarpoolcovers

2) Solar Sun Ring - Solar sun rings are manageable 5 foot discs made from UV resistant, high-quality vinyl that floats on your pool's surface. They come in packages of one or more rings so that you have enough to cover the surface of your pool. They join themselves together with built in magnets on their outer rings. This makes it easy to pull apart and remove from the pool without it being one large heavy cover. One person alone can do it as they're so easy to manage.

Their upper clear layer holds insulating air and focuses sunlight on its lower blue layer. They are strong and durable and can absorb about 50%

of sunlight and convert it into heat while letting the rest of the sunlight pass into the pool for deeper water heating, thus raising the temperature of the pool. And they are quite inexpensive and last a long time. If you've never seen what they look like, look at the ones Amazon has at www.livesmartinfo.com/solarsunrings

3) SolarPill - Liquid Solar Blanket - It's amazing how this works! You almost can't believe that it even works; but it does. Basically it's a container of thermally insulating liquid that you poor into your swimming pool and it slowly spreads itself out thinly on the surface of the pool forming an invisible layer of non-toxic, biodegradable, harmless film that reduces water evaporation and traps heat which saves energy.

One SolarPill (or capsule) for every 30,000 gallons lasts up to one month, 24 hours a day. It won't affect the chemical balance of chlorine, mineral sanitizers, salt water or automatic pool cleaners. It's safe for you and the environment so of course you can be in the pool while it's in there. After everyone leaves the pool, the liquid comes together again and reforms the protective film.

This is the easiest alternative to using a physical pool cover because there's nothing to remove or cover.

You can find any of these items at your swimming pool supplies store. But if you would like to see what the containers look like at Amazon, you can see them at www.livesmartinfo.com/solarpill

To wrap things up, solar power can make for true sustainability if you're able to get your system set up. The energy is so clean and natural and won't run out. Any part of it that you're in a position to take advantage of is something wonderful to do for the environment.

RESOURCES

1. http://www.nrel.gov/gis/solar.html

Additionally, for great information on solar PV costs along with many charts and statistics, take a look at: http://eetd.lbl.gov/ea/emp/reports/lbnl-5047e.pdf

C H A P T E R ~10~

HYBRID ELECTRIC VEHICLES - WHAT YOU SHOULD KNOW ABOUT THEM!

Although we are at least a dozen years into the 21st century, people are still unsure how hybrid cars actually work. That, among other factors we will consider, plays a role in holding people back from getting into one. New technology is constantly coming out, so people get confused. There are definitely pros and cons where this is concerned. So let's get some clarification and insight into what a hybrid car is - which is sometimes referred to as an "electric vehicle" or EV (although it's a hybrid). You see . . . it's starting already.

What Is a Hybrid Car (aka Hybrid Electric Vehicle "HEV")?

Think of the word "hybrid" as a combination of two. To keep it simple, a hybrid car is a combination of an electric powered engine and a gasoline powered engine built into *one* car that's engineered to be more efficient; around 70% less in terms of greenhouse gases. Reducing emissions, car exhaust fumes and carbon footprint promotes a cleaner environment. That is partially why those interested in going green take such an interest in this type of vehicle. However, a hybrid car's fuel efficiency is *the* main reason why interest in this vehicle is so high; considering the cost of gasoline.

Caution - You don't want to get "hybrid" vehicles confused with "all-electric" vehicles because there is a difference. An all-electric vehicle totally operates on rechargeable battery power alone and uses no gas at all to run. So unlike a hybrid vehicle, there is no gas tank.

Some Hybrid vehicles can go +/-100 miles per hour and can get up to 50 miles per gallon around town; depending on the make and model which varies. That's just to give you an idea of how fast they can go. If you're interested in an SUV hybrid because maybe you need more space or have kids, etc., those are available as well but they do not get as many miles per gallon and they aren't the best choice for off-roading.

How Does A Hybrid Vehicle Work?

Using computer technology, the electric and gas engines play off each other to decipher which one to engage. For instance, if you're driving on surface streets and not in a hurry to be somewhere or if you're in traffic sitting around just stopping and going, which means you're not driving much, the electric engine will engage. In contrast to that, if you're driving an open road or the freeway for a while at higher speeds, the gas engine will dominate. Also, if you need to drive up a hill or accelerate, the electric engine gives the car extra power which takes stress (or pressure) off the car and that saves gas. Transitioning from electric to gas or vice versa is quite smooth as the two propulsion systems are designed to work in harmony together; which gives the driver a good driving experience.

There's also an auto-stop feature which means the electric engine takes control so that the car does not idle at a red light. However, when the light turns green and you put your foot on the accelerator, the combustion engine has to re-engage which can take about a second or so. If you think that's going to irritate you or slow you down, make sure this is something you want to deal with.

Just a side note, there's a special oil that hybrid cars use. So if you are unable to take it to the dealership or a service center where they have this oil in stock, be sure to keep some on hand so that you can have it readily available in the event you need it. I mention this because not every car repair place can properly service hybrid vehicles at this time. But the more popular they become, the more places there will be to service them.

One of the things that take away from the hybrid car's efficiency is the weight of the battery pack. It's large, takes up a lot of space and is heavy, at least the first generation models; plus you've got the electric engine as well. So when it's being powered by the gas engine, it has a lot more weight to lug around which requires more gas rendering it less efficient in that regard.

If you personally have not driven an HEV even for a test drive, it's important to do so because there's a different feel going on than what you've been used to in a 100% gasoline combustion engine. Also, if you're in the market for a hybrid vehicle, you'll want to seriously consider the information mentioned here.

Hybrid Car Batteries

There are 3 different types of hybrid car batteries. The first and worst one, which is on its way out, is the **lead-acid battery** because it's the most toxic; plus it's huge and heavy, rendering it non-efficient. The second one is the **nickel-metal hydride (aka "NiMH")** which is a second-generation battery for many hybrid cars. Finally the third battery is the **lithium-ion (aka "Li-ion")** which in comparison to the other two has higher energy density and is the least toxic. It is the most efficient; rendering it the battery of choice for hybrid manufacturers at this time.

Hybrid car batteries recharge themselves by the combustion engine, so there's no need to plug them in. How it works is when the engine runs, the charger spins and gives it current which charges the battery. This usually happens when you're coasting or braking.

If you're wondering how long a hybrid car battery lasts, well, it could be close to the life of the car. But you do get a pretty reasonable manufacturer warranty of give or take 10 years or 100,000 miles. But it should be good for longer than that. The Toyota Prius has been out for over a decade now and only about 500 NiMH battery packs have expired (see Resource #1). So that goes to show the longevity of these rechargeable batteries.

In a rare case that you do need to replace the full battery pack, it can cost around $3,000 or more. However, about 1% of hybrid vehicles are currently on the road worldwide (see Resource #2). But it's growing and some of them were even on order at one point. So eventually, refurbished or used batteries will become more readily available and you'll be able to buy one at a more practical cost; especially if the car has been in an accident with an intact battery still in place. Who knows - In the future, perhaps there will be laptop and cellphone type batteries for hybrids!

In regards to recycling programs, the various EV manufacturers have a company that they use for recycling dead batteries thus keeping them out of landfills.

'Plug-In' Hybrid Electric Vehicles (aka "PHEV")

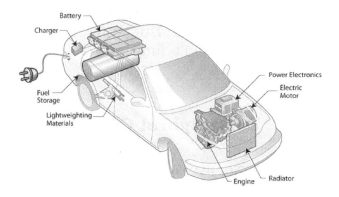

Courtesy of Matt Howard

Plug-in hybrid vehicles combine features of the regular hybrid vehicle and the electric vehicle ("EV"). This means they can strictly run on batteries like the EV because of their electric engine; yet they can use gasoline like a hybrid because of their combustion engine.

Unlike a hybrid electric vehicle (HEV) where the gas engine provides its power, the plug-in hybrid's power *mainly* comes from its electric engine and the gas engine is primarily for its reserves. This means PHEVs must be plugged into an electric power supply to be recharged daily (overnight for a complete charge) thus giving you longer use of a "full" charge so that you can drive farther without having to use up your gas; especially for daily commuting. This helps reduce greenhouse gases to a higher degree than regular HEVs; not to mention it saves you gasoline money too.

This is a great website to see a list of PHEVs that are currently available now: http://www.pluginamerica.org/vehicles. But at this time, HEVs dominate the market because it self-recharges allowing it to drive locally or long distance. The most popular one is the Prius. However there are many others and more are coming. Yes, the Toyota Prius paved the way and is the "granddaddy" hybrid. But it is not the only player out there so don't limit yourself to explore others.

Used Hybrid Cars

Now that we are more than a decade into hybrid cars, the market for used hybrids is picking up including for used hybrid SUVs. Owners want to get into newer models and be a part of the latest generation with the finest technology. As gas prices keep heading north, it becomes more of a viable option.

It goes without saying that you're going to pay less for any kind of used vehicle so hybrids are no different except that they really do hold their value. However, before purchasing a pre-owned hybrid, there's a lot of research that should be done to make sure you're getting what you "think" you are getting.

A good place to start is with a CarFax Vehicle History report. It'll tell you all kinds of things particularly if the car has ever been in an accident. This is extremely important if you are looking to buy a used hybrid from a dealership because they fix up cars to look so nice like brand new. So it's hard to tell what that car gas gone through before it got to their lot. It is YOUR responsibility to investigate that information and be in the know. Get comfortable doing research online to get additional suggestions as to pertinent questions you should be asking the seller including crucial warranty information when it comes to hybrids. This advice applies when you're buying from a private party as well.

To sum it up, there are lots of different makes and models of hybrid cars out on the market today and more are forthcoming. It's true that they cost more than regular non-hybrids in their class so the upfront cost does play a role in people's decision to buy one. Some hybrid vehicle owners even feel that the supposed savings in the long run isn't worth the upfront cost. That's something you'll have to decide for yourself. But technology is progressively improving for these types of vehicles and the price will steadily come down so that it's feasible for more of the population to own one, and consumer demand will grow. What a great way to take a toll off the environment and your fuel expense!

RESOURCES:

1. http://www.greencarreports.com/news/1071
   391_life-after-death-what-happens-when-
   your-prius-battery-dies
2. http://www.businessweek.com/ap/financialn
   ews/D9RGK6C00.htm

CHAPTER ~11~

MAGNETIC ELECTRICITY FOR SUSTAINABLE LIVING

Continuing on the subject of green energy and sustainable living, we don't want to leave out magnetic power as a source of renewable energy. There is not as much awareness of this energy source like there is with solar and wind power; at least not yet. But electricity can be made with the use of magnets. However, a magnetic electricity generator (aka MEG) would have to be built in order to create that power which in turn generates electricity that can be used in the home and help to lower the electricity bill. Don't confuse it with electromagnetic energy which is when an electrical current is sent through a coil of wire thus magnetizing it. As with the others, it's clean, eco-friendly and produces no air pollution.

What Is A Magnetic Electric Generator And How Does It Work?

A magnetic power generator is a system that uses the power of magnets to produce electricity which occurs when the magnetic forces push against each other within the generator. The stronger the magnetic force (or push), the more energy that is produced. It is a perpetual machine which means once it starts spinning it won't stop (unless the magnets are removed from their positions). As long as the magnets keep attracting and repulsing, energy will continue to be generated. This motion is self-powered by the magnets, so considering magnets do not exhaust their inherent power, the generators continuously rotate and produce electric power.

In regards to magnetic power generation, the MEG needs to power itself first before it can start powering anything else. So there's a certain waiting period after it starts before electricity is made depending on its size. Also, the size of the magnets determines the amount of electricity it produces which affects the magnetic force. So the larger the size and weight, the more electricity produced.

A battery power pack is needed to spark a magnetic electricity generator into motion which is why some negate the claim that it has no combustibility and runs on its own power. But to clear that up, it's just a car battery that last at least 5 years that's needed and it is not a spark but a dry cell transport to the generator. This means there is never a flammable start procedure or a spark as there is in a car or lawn mower engine. Rather, it is the energy produced by the magnets on their own that gives power to the rotating turbine which drives the electricity through the home. Polarity is a special characteristic of magnets which makes them work continuously. It is that continuous motion that forces the internal turbines to keep moving and produce electric power.

What Should I Know About Building A Do-It-Yourself (DIY) Meg To Generate Electricity?

These magnetic electric generators apparently are not very difficult to build as they require no special technique or special tools outside of what you probably already have in your tool box. A basic small unit does not take up much space and can be built in less than a day; of course depending on how avid of a do-it-yourselfer you are. The electric parts that are used to build it can be found at a hardware store and it can cost around $100. If you're trying to save money, buying a readymade MEG certainly would cost a lot more, which is why people opt to simply build one themselves. It can possibly save you about 30% on energy bills. But you can build more than one (because they're not that large) for further savings.

You will definitely need a proper DIY instruction manual or guide so that you know exactly how to do it which will have visuals, all the details; the usual. If you want to know more about it, there's lots of information online or you can take a look here: www.livesmartinfo.com/meg

To wrap things up, what's nice about magnetic energy generators is that they can generate electricity regardless of the earth's temperature or the weather condition. Solar electricity is influenced by having enough sunlight. Wind turbines do not rotate if there is no wind to push them to generate power. But for magnetic energy generators, its source of power is internal which means outside factors do not influence its electricity production. So any place in the world is fair game to have one. As far as noise level, it's no different from any other energy device such as a water heater or oil burner. Aside from that, using a MEG as an alternative energy resource for generating electricity could be a viable option.

SHORT CONCLUSION

In conclusion, the ever-increasing focus on sustainable living has extended to virtually every aspect of our existence. Compliance requirements vary from one country to another. A wealth of informational resources is available online and urged to look deeper into for further enlightenment.

Voluntary participation in taking action to reduce one's carbon footprint is highly encouraged. You can go green without greenwashing yourself. Within your means, sustainable living can be brought to fruition for you and your family.

Please share with information with others because the more people that become aware and take action, the better it will be for our environment and planet!